4/01

D0365750

Earl Coon

 St. Louis Community College

Forest Park
Florissant Valley
Meramec

Instructional Resources
St. Louis, Missouri

GAYLORD S

CULTURE WARS
AND THE
GLOBAL VILLAGE

CULTURE WARS
AND THE
GLOBAL VILLAGE
A DIPLOMAT'S PERSPECTIVE
CARL COON

PB Prometheus Books

59 John Glenn Drive
Amherst, New York 14228-2197

Published 2000 by Prometheus Books

Inquiries should be addressed to
Prometheus Books
59 John Glenn Drive
Amherst, New York 14228–2197
VOICE: 716–691–0133, ext. 207
FAX: 716–564–2711
WWW.PROMETHEUSBOOKS.COM

04 03 02 01 00   5 4 3 2 1

Library of Congress Cataloging-in-Publication Data

Coon, Carleton S. (Carleton Stevens), 1927–
    Culture wars and the global village : a diplomat's perspective / Carl
Coon.
        p. cm.
    Includes bibliographical references and index.
    ISBN 1–57392–801–1 (cloth : alk. paper)
    1. Cultural relativism. 2. Intercultural communication. 3. Pluralism
(Social sciences). 4. Communication and culture. 5. Civilization, Modern—
1950– I. Title.

GN345.5 .C66 2000
306—dc21   99–045207
                                                                 CIP

Printed in the United States of America on acid-free paper

CONTENTS

PART II: FOREGROUND

INTRODUCTION

T he first part of this book is about cultures. I define the
term to mean the distinctive mental habits that bond individuals
to their group, and persuade them that they are different from
other groups. I mean the particular assemblages of ethnic, linguistic, religious, ethical, and other behavioral features that distinguish Kurds from Arabs or Serbs from Albanians or Tutsi
from Hutu. I mean the sense of belonging, the shared feeling of
being a member of an in-group, that provides the individual
with a sense of identity. I mean the kind of coherent, homogeneous social unit within which people find their identity, and for
which many people are still willing to fight.

In many of the world's countries, internal cultural distinctions are blending into larger, more inclusive societies. The

United States is a prime example. Here, the signposts are available for anyone to see. Ethnic jokes and put-downs, for example, are socially unacceptable. Young people address each other by their first names only. The nature-nurture debate has for a couple of generations been biased in favor of the nurturists. It's all part of the same pattern: a blurring of former group distinctions based on religion or accent or country of origin in favor of a sense of belonging to an enlarged community comprising the whole nation. It is a major step forward in a process that has been going on for millennia: the gradual evolution of human societies in the direction of ever larger and more complex units.

This ongoing process of assimilation is laudable, but it makes it hard for many of us to understand where we are coming from, the roots and soil from which we have grown. We see conflict in the Balkans or Central Africa from the outside, and deplore it without understanding it. I want to offer some concepts that hopefully will contribute to a higher level of understanding. Specifically:

1. During the long period of the Paleolithic Era, social organization was limited mainly to small hunter-gatherer tribes. This was the incubation period for what we now know as human nature.

2. The development of agriculture and animal husbandry catapulted humanity onto a new level. Problems of individual versus group interests became acute as the groups became larger and their ways of life more complex. Cultures added new religious practices and ethical strictures to help people adjust to evolving technologies.

3. Competition intensified between culturally defined groups of people for land and other resources. Frequently this competition ended in conflict, with the advantage going to the group with the stronger internal bonds, the one that could com-

mand the most intense loyalty from its people. Contemporary conflicts in places like the Middle East and the Balkans involve the survivors of this kind of evolutionary process, one that has been going on since ancient times.

4. Strong internal bonds were not always decisive, however. Successful groups tended to grow larger and more complex. When a larger and more complex group collided with a smaller one, the former usually prevailed. Thus the gradual trend of human societies to grow larger, more inclusive, and more technologically advanced can also be seen as the outcome of an evolutionary process.

5. Our planet is finite, and the limits of human social evolution through competition between cultures have been reached. The largest and most complex societies are multicultural, or are fast becoming so. Culture is no longer the dominant criterion for group selection. Conflicts between cultures still produce sparks in some places, but the era when they were the prime engine of social evolution is ending.

6. Human society is in the middle of the most profoundly disorienting transition since the dawn of the Neolithic. A new panhumanist ethos is dawning that recognizes the essential oneness of all humanity. Global population and environmental problems have become critical, accompanied by the multiple problems of how human society as a whole can organize itself to cope with a truly new situation.

As we struggle with the symptoms of this massive change in our condition, we need all the understanding we can muster about where we are coming from and how we arrived here. We can reject old-fashioned "Social Darwinism" and still recognize that for millennia, conflict between culturally defined groups played a dominant role in the way our history and prehistory unfolded. We now have the tools to understand where we came from, and be liberated and strengthened by that knowledge. The modern individual goes on from there to internalize the recognition that we are all one species, and from now on the need is for cooperation, not conflict, on a global scale.

And having learned that lesson, we need to focus on new priorities, based on a fresh assessment of human society and its relation to our planet. That is what the second half of this book is about.

In a way, I started preparing to write this book a half century ago, when I decided, at age twenty-two, to join the U.S. Foreign Service. I had already traveled and lived abroad enough to know that my main interest in life was people: other people; people who dressed, worshiped, and thought in different ways. I wanted to understand other societies in depth and in the round. I wanted to be more than a tourist. The Foreign Service offered me an opportunity to live long enough in one place to get under the surface and understand the local culture, and then move on. I was fortunate, in that the assignment process allowed me to live for several years each in Germany, Morocco, Syria, Iran, India, and Nepal. In between, and during these assignments, I traveled widely in other regions. I suppose you could say I have the wanderlust; since retirement I have traveled to many other regions, like Central Asia and Latin America, that I missed during my active service.

Before I would get to a new post I would bone up on the geography, history, social structure, and literature of the target area, plus any other background that seemed relevant. Perhaps I'd read a novel or two by a local author. After my arrival I would start what you might call the lab phase. I would seek out and cultivate bicultural individuals sensitive to cross-cultural nuances and willing to explain them to me. I would travel around the area as much as I could. I would observe, collate, and gradually assemble a practical working understanding of the prevalent attitudes, values, and concerns, particularly the ones that differed from those in my country.

My primary motive was curiosity, but the results of my efforts paid both immediate and long-term dividends. In the short term I was more effective as a diplomat. If Washington wanted me to make a point, I knew how to put it. When the locals wanted to make a point to my government, I knew how to interpret it.

In the longer term, I gradually assembled a kind of data base about all the wonderfully varied ways people's minds worked in the different environments I had come to understand. I began to correlate similarities and differences across cultures. Patterns began to emerge. Then I retired and started reading about evolution, and things fell into place. The result is this book.

Many historians, philosophers, and others have followed different paths as they attempted to explain the ways our human societies have changed. I have no argument with them, no desire to replace their perceptions with an alternative theory of my own. I have no quarrel with Arnold Toynbee or Max Weber, or for that matter with Karl Marx or John Kenneth Galbraith. They each have contributed to the sum total of human understanding; they and many others like them have been the principal architects of the conceptual frameworks through which people have come to understand who they are and how they came to be. The concepts I propose in this book are designed not to dispute them but to provide another perspective. I am trying to supplement, not displace.

No conceptual effort like this book arises in a vacuum. I've drawn on more than my own experiences and the books I've cited in footnotes. I have shamelessly exploited the advice and help of friends, too numerous to cite here. But I would particularly like to thank Sue Blackmore, Lindsey Grant, Ned Hall, Robert Hinde (Cambridge), Scott Miller, Margaret Nydell (Georgetown), Suzanne Olds, Ted Riccardi (Columbia), and Pete Richerson (University of California/Davis). Special thanks go to my severest critic, my wife, Jane.

PART I
BACKGROUND

CHAPTER 1

FROM MY GALLERY OF CULTURAL SNAPSHOTS

T he following four anecdotes, drawn from my personal experience, can help explain where I am coming from when I theorize about human nature and cultural groups.

END OF AN ERA:
THE MONKEY HUNTERS

Progress usually carries a price. A major price humanity is paying in the present era is the snuffing out of cultural diversity at the more primitive end of the scale. Small, tribal-sized hunter-gatherer societies still existed in many out-of-the-way places around the habitable world a century ago, but they are van-

15

ishing, for the most part, like puddles of water on hot pavement. They are being absorbed into larger and more complex cultures, or they are simply dying, the will to survive having been dampened by adversity and hopelessness to the point they no longer have the will to continue. I am not an anthropologist, but my father was, and thanks to him I was at least aware of many such groups, and occasionally I came across one of them myself. Let's start our walk through my cultural memories with this snapshot of a very small culture in the process of expiring.

From 1956 to 1959 I was assigned to our embassy in New Delhi, India. In January 1957, I visited Dr. B. S. Guha, head of the Tribal Research Institute in Ranchi, Bihar. My father was visiting and provided the excuse; he and Guha were old friends and colleagues, both of them eminent and controversial anthropologists. Guha's Institute was in charge of a large area of so-called reserved land, reserved that is for the aboriginal tribes that lived in the jungle there. The arrangement was somewhat similar to our Indian reservations, except that the aborigines were for the most part less affected by modern societies than our Native Americans and the arrangements were more paternalistic. Guha was actively engaged in efforts to bring the aborigines under his supervision into the modern world. It was a lonely and difficult task. He was glad to see us.

We found ourselves driving on a gravel road through dense jungle in Guha's old Hudson. Suddenly he put on the brakes, as we approached a ragtag collection of tepeelike huts and lean-tos in a clearing a little way off the road. "Birhor," he said, "the last tribe we haven't settled. They wander all over the jungle, and I've been looking for them." We got out and looked over the encampment. Naked babies, mothers nursing, children running around, and a couple of young men loafing, all clad in rags. It didn't look that different on the surface from an urban slum in

Calcutta, except that it was out in the jungle, and the shelters were made entirely from local jungle vegetation. Guha marched over to one of the huts and, squatting, engaged an elderly man in serious conversation in what sounded to me like a kind of pidgin Hindi. After a while Guha rose and we continued our journey. "Well, that does it," he said. "This tribe has been resisting our efforts to get it to settle down and take up farming, but their chief just told me he and his people were willing to go along with our plans. We'll have them settled soon enough now."

I have no idea how long the Birhor had lived in that jungle as hunter-gatherers, and I doubt whether anyone else knows either. Seminomadic, they were skilled at making ropes out of vines and nets out of the ropes. They placed their nets at strategic places and drove monkeys into them, then killed and ate their prey. This plus whatever vegetable products they could glean from the jungle constituted their food supply. They had a few metal tools that they had somehow managed to import from the outside world but aside from that their lifestyle had changed little from that of their ancestors. They had probably been there, living that lifestyle, for many generations before the Gautama Buddha was born a few score miles away, 2,500 years ago. They would still be there now, if the tidal wave of modern civilization had passed them by. I was there at the moment of engulfment.

There's another small tribe that still maintains the old lifestyle in the central Terai region of Nepal, a couple of hundred miles north of Ranchi, and just south of the massive Himalayan mountain range. A small, shy, and elusive band called the Raute ("row-tay") keep very much to themselves in that remote area, so much so that they hardly ever communicate even with local villagers. The Raute, like the Birhor, are monkey hunters. Perhaps their ancestors, and those of the Birhor, roamed in the jungle that used to stretch in an uninterrupted belt throughout much of northern India. If so, there were probably a lot more of them then, but as civilization encroached on their environment, and the jungle gave way to rice paddies, roads, and villages, their numbers diminished, to the present vanishing point.

Peoples like the Birhor and the Raute find it very difficult to assimilate into modern cultures. The gap is too great. When confronted with what we call civilization, most of them usually die of modern diseases for which they have no natural immunities. The survivors may then drift to cities, where they form an underclass below the existing underclasses, living in utmost squalor. After we left Ranchi we visited the neighboring steel town of Jamshedpur where we saw some of this human driftwood, urbanized refugees from the jungle hanging around on street corners, usually drunk. They seemed animated only by a desire to get their hands on cheap liquor and drown their memories in a bottle.

The Tribal Research Institute represented a sincere effort by the government of India to help these people make the transition, and Guha was an excellent choice to run the Ranchi program. But it wasn't working very well. After we left the Birhor, Guha drove us farther into the reserved area where another tribe, the Asur ("ah-soor"), had been settled. Guha's predecessor, under government instructions, had set them up as beekeepers. There were lots of beehives, and enough farmland to allow them to grow much of their own food. They were happy to see Guha, trotted out enormous quantities of their homemade beer, and celebrated with dancing and singing that lasted most of the day. In the end they gave us two jars of honey, explaining that that was their total year's crop—the government having failed to check on whether there were any flowers in the region before settling them there. There were almost no flowers, so the bees rushed around without producing much of anything to show for their labor. Guha kept one jar, I kept the other. It was delicious.

There are exceptions, when a tribal culture can find a niche in modern society and survive, for a while at least. Some Native American tribes in the United States have taken advantage of old treaty rights to set up profitable gambling casinos. Likewise, some of India's tribal monkey hunters, I've been told, turned their Stone Age skills to advantage by capturing monkeys alive, for export to Western research laboratories. Indian public opinion strongly opposed this kind of commerce and the government's attitude was quite ambivalent, but there was money in the trade and one hopes the hunters received at least a small portion of it.

CULTURAL EVOLUTION: FIRST LIGHT IN THE HIMALAYAS

Most Americans don't realize that Nepal's population is racially mixed and culturally diverse. There is a basic ethnic/linguistic cleavage between Mongoloid peoples who came in originally from the east and north, and Indo-European groups who entered from the south and west. The latter speak Nepali, a close relative of Hindi, as their native language, and are Hindus, divided into castes. Most of them are Brahmins (priestly caste) or Chhetris (warrior caste). The Mongoloid tribespeople speak a variety of languages and are divided into tribal groups, e.g., the Gurung, the Magar, and the Limbu, to name a few. They are relatively unconcerned with caste distinctions. And then there are the Newar, the original inhabitants of the Kathmandu valley, who have been there so long, and are of such mixed origin, that they occupy a category by themselves.

Technically, the Nepali word "jat" translates as "caste," but in common parlance it identifies caste only if the person involved is a Nepali speaker of Indo-European stock; if you ask a Gurung what his "jat" is, he'll say simply that he is a Gurung and leave it at that.

I was first posted to Kathmandu in 1970, and started right away to explore this cultural diversity. I took many walks around the edges of the beautiful valley of Kathmandu, where trails wind up to hill villages. My friend, interpreter, and principal informant, Bir Bahadur Adhikari, usually accompanied me. He is from the eastern hills region and is a Chhetri Hindu. I used to try to identify hillsmen walking up or down the trails by their dress and physical appearance and manner, and soon I got to be pretty good at it. Bir would check by stopping the individual and asking him flat out: "Apke jat ke ho?" ("What is your jat?"). This would provoke a big smile and a cheerful reply: Brahmin, or Gurung, or whatever. Then Bir would have a sociable little chat, and find out about the man's family and business, and we would part on the best of terms. I don't know why, but Nepali hill people are among the most gregarious and friendly people on earth. Bir's query, which wouldn't fly in the United States at all, never produced the slightest sign of hostility in his interlocutor.

Until one day, that is, when we stopped a young Nepali man, dressed in Nepali national dress, coming into town. "What is your jat?" "I am a Nepali." "Yes, but what is your *jat*?" "I am a Nepali citizen, that's all. And that's enough." Bir was astounded, dumbstruck by this unprecedented response. And I thought to myself, Well, maybe there's some hope for this country, after all.

COUNTERPOINT: FROZEN ISLANDS

The British, an insular people themselves, have had a lot of experience in managing other people's islands. They started with Ireland, went on to Ceylon (now Sri Lanka), and eventually took over the administration of Cyprus. All three remain embroiled in bitter conflict between culturally defined groups, long after the British Raj departed. In each case, one must conclude that either the Brits didn't know what they were letting themselves in for, or that their colonial leaders were slow learners.

Take the case of Cyprus, where the population is 80 percent Greek and 20 percent Turkish. At least, it was when I became the Cyprus desk officer in the State Department in 1961. One of the first things I did was to visit the Cypriot embassy in Washington and call on the charge d'affaires, an amiable Turkish diplomat. He introduced me to his Greek subordinate. Ambassador Rossides, a Greek Cypriot, maintained his official residence in New York, where he served as ambassador to the United Nations, and only visited his Washington embassy occasionally. When he did, then of course he was in charge.

Several weeks later I called at the embassy again, to visit the charge d'affaires. This time it was the Greek. The Turk, who had been in charge during my first visit, had been temporarily demoted; he was now his former subordinate's subordinate, and was nowhere to be seen. It seems that Ambassador Rossides was not in New York, he was out of the country, consulting back in Nicosia. The arrangement was as follows: between Washington and New York, there should always be one mission run by a Greek and one by a Turk. In each post the ambassador's senior deputy was a Turk, so the arrangement worked, as long as he was one place or the other. But while he was outside the

United States, and in charge of neither post, the Greek in Washington had to be somersaulted over the head of his Turkish boss, for otherwise you would have the intolerable situation of having a Turk in charge of each of the two posts.

It is such exquisite attention to detail that has given durability to the so-called Cyprus problem, where hostility between the island's Greek and Turkish populations has continued to this day, threatening not only peace on the island, but relations between Greece and Turkey. Time after time, well-meaning foreign powers have tried to create a genuine peace on that beautiful but unhappy island, only to see their efforts founder on the deep hatred and mistrust these two communities harbor for each other.

RELIGION IN SYRIA

In the summer of 1952 the State Department assigned me to Damascus, Syria. Soon after I started working at the embassy, I hired a gentleman named Michel Husseini to help me brush up my French, and then start studying Arabic. Michel was a Lebanese Christian, and he had spent his active career, twenty years or so, teaching at a lycee or high school in Damascus. An intense person, he was dedicated to his teaching and pounded classical Arabic into me with a determination approaching ferocity. Eventually, however, I realized that the Arabic he was teaching me bore no more relationship to the Arabic I was hearing on the streets than Latin does to French. So I asked him if he could lighten up a bit, give me some instruction in modern vernacular Damascene. He bridled, and stated that he wanted me to speak a form of Arabic so "pure" that it would put to shame the ignoramuses of this terrible town of Damascus. We never did work the matter out, and I never did get to use the Arabic I learned from him, except once in Afghanistan, talking to a mullah—but that is another story.

One day he was late for our lesson, unusual for him, and I went to the front landing to see if I could see him on the street. Across the street was a police wagon and a group of hushed bystanders. Michel was among them; he saw me and came over. His face was long, his body language that of a mourner at a funeral. "What happened?" I asked. "Ah," he said, "a terrible thing has just occurred. One of my students failed his baccalaureate exam. His father is the police chief and keeps his revolver in his desk. The boy knew about it, and came home and got the revolver." Michel put his finger to his temple, and with contorted features pressed an imaginary trigger. "Bang," he said tragically. "He blew his brains out." "How awful," I said. "Tell me about him. What kind of a boy was he?"

As soon as he focused on the quality of the late lamented, as opposed to the fact of his demise, Husseini's mobile Arab features underwent a remarkable transformation. No longer any trace of the mourner, he was triumphant, even gleeful. "Ho ho," he announced, "he was a Muslim."

In one plangent instant, I learned the true meaning of communalism in the Middle East.

CHAPTER 2

THE BIOLOGICAL EVOLUTION OF HUMANKIND

This whole book is based on the belief that Darwin was right and the creationists are wrong. Evolution as first defined in its modern form by Darwin provides a reasoned explanation of how our planet came to be populated by all the living creatures we see around us. It provides a plausible account of how thinking human beings like us first arrived. It accommodates an ever-expanding body of biological evidence, economically and without requiring major adjustments. It accepts with equal grace the additional evidence coming in from relatively new life sciences like genetics. And, most important of all, it does not ask us to assume the existence of a superior intelligence, a Creator. To do that, we would have to accept as fact something that is inherently unverifiable. We don't have to make a leap of faith to accept evolution; we simply have to observe the world around us and exercise our reason.

One essential feature of the Darwinian approach is that evolution does *not* have a higher purpose or a built-in direction. There is no architect with an end in view, building up increasingly complex forms of life toward some preconceived objective. The directions evolution takes result from an almost infinitely large number of very small events. The past is fixed, because it has happened, but the future is inherently unknowable, because it is being determined in the present, by everything that is happening now.

While evolution does not have a purpose, it is a process that operates according to an underlying principle, which can be summed up as follows: *all life evolves by the differential survival of replicating entities.*[1] The first requirement is an entity that is capable of replicating itself. Put it in an environment where it can survive and replicate and pretty soon you have many copies. They are not all exact copies; a little variation creeps in over time. As soon as the total population starts to outrun the food supply, or the available space, natural selection takes over. The individual organisms that have some advantage over the others—even if the advantage is very slight—will have somewhat better chances of replicating themselves and, over the course of thousands of generations, the better-adapted types will predominate.

In order to understand how the multiplicity of flora and fauna now on the planet could have evolved in this manner, one has to internalize the enormous amounts of time that have elapsed since life first began. If there are ten million fruit flies, and only one in each ten generations happens to be born with a selective advantage, like an eye or other sense organ that works a little better, then over a million generations there will have been at least a hundred thousand of them breeding and transmitting their particular genetic advantage. A million generations for the fruit fly is nothing compared to the many millions of years during which that species has been evolving. Or take an example closer to home: If every one of our remote ancestors migrated only ten miles away from where he was born, then in a thousand generations his progeny could have spread out ten thousand miles. Twenty thousand years, a thousand generations, is not long in the history of our species.

HOW NATURAL SELECTION WORKS

Several years ago I had the good fortune to visit the forest of Bialowiecza in eastern Poland. It is unique in that it is the only substantial tract of genuinely virgin forest in all of Europe.[2] And what a difference! As I walked through it, accompanied by an able guide, I saw a bewildering variety of plant forms that had specialized and adapted to imperceptible variations in soil, proximity to water, microclimatology, and other variables. Over tens of thousands of years, natural selection had operated at increasingly subtle levels, with each refinement opening up the possibility of still more highly specialized ones. There are thousands of plant species in Bialowiecza that simply do not exist anyplace else. No other temperate forest I've ever seen could match its variety. It was like the Library of Congress compared to your corner bookstore. It gave new meaning to the term "climax vegetation."

Was the climax vegetation in Bialowiecza in a true state of equilibrium? Had it "arrived" and reached a degree of perfection beyond which further change, further adaptation was inconceivable? Of course not. There is no such thing as absolute perfection in our biosphere. Climax vegetation signifies a condition where natural selection has run its course for a long time under stable environmental conditions, and the rate of change has correspondingly slowed down and moved from the macro- to the microlevel. The norm, particularly in the modern era, is for unstable environments placing stress on existing life-forms and demanding correspondingly high rates of adaptive change.

The environment may change for geological or climatic reasons. Normally such changes occur only over a long period of time. Events like the extinction of the dinosaurs, evidently from the fallout of a massive meteor impact, are the exception rather than the rule. The vegetation at Bialowiecza was presumably quite different during the Ice Ages, but it had a long period of environmental stability since then to flourish and become more specialized. Sometimes, however, the environment may change relatively rapidly. Such change usually results from changes in the biosphere itself. When natural selection, based on the differential survival of replicating entities, produces entities better adapted to a given environment, that environment will also be changed by their presence. The changes so effected may be minimal, as for example when a butterfly arrives on the scene with a new kind of wing pattern. But the changes can also be catastrophic. In recent decades, human population pressures have caused the extinction of many species of plants and animals.

There is a rhythm here, a kind of oscillating principle that constitutes the warp and woof of the tapestry of all life on our planet. Life-forms and the environment are dancing together, changing each other as they themselves change. The tempo speeds up when environmental changes open up opportunities for major new adaptations, and slows down when the ideal of a "climax" population is approached. But it never stops entirely; the dance goes on.

That tempo was seldom more than a stately andante before *Homo sapiens* appeared on the scene, but then it began to accelerate. The accelerando was gradual during the Paleolithic period, but picked up speed more rapidly since then. Now it is prestissimo, with human-caused impacts on the environment thrusting changes on every part of the biosphere at an unprecedented rate, while those same changes present humanity with a bewildering array of new challenges.

CONFLICTING EVIDENCE ON HUMAN ORIGINS

The question of how humans originated has fascinated people since the beginning of recorded thought, and probably for a long time before. Origin myths constitute some of the richest folklore of the hunter-gatherer societies that have survived into modern times. And for all our sophistication, contemporary scientists and philosophers are still arguing about when and where and how our sapient ancestors originated. The most important issue at present arises from a serious conflict between the available archeological evidence and relatively recent evidence gleaned from genetic studies.

The scientific community has accumulated an interesting array of bones and stones and other tangible evidence of the kinds of animals our remote hominid cousins were, enough to engender various theories about how our chimplike ancestors changed and became more human. But there isn't nearly enough to establish a clear lineage in a definitive way. We have similarly spotty evidence from various parts of the world showing that the immediate predecessors of modern humans were a subspecies we have chosen to call *Homo erectus*, distinguished from *Homo sapiens* mainly by a smaller brain size and a bigger jaw. The earliest skeletal remains that are clearly *erectus* go back perhaps a million and a half years. The evidence for *Homo sapiens*, by contrast, suggests an earliest date of perhaps about 300,000 years, and even that is arguable.[3]

Interestingly, some of the finer details of the skeletal remains of *erectus* vary regionally in ways that resemble regional racial variations in modern people. This evidence suggests that *H. erectus* may have evolved into *H. sapiens* more than once, in more than one place. Race, it would appear, may be older than we are; it may antedate the dawn of modern people and go far back into the remote past.[4]

But now the geneticists are weighing in. Recent breakthroughs in their studies have made possible a new approach to ascertaining lineages, including those of humans, through the study of that portion of human genetic material that is known as "mitochondrial DNA."[5] This has led to a conclusion that is strikingly different from what the archeological evidence suggests: all living humans are descended from a single African female who lived about 130,000 years ago.

Understandably the controversy here is hot and heavy. Majority opinion has favored the so-called radiation theory based on the genetic evidence, but a growing minority questions whether it cannot be reconciled with some version of the older theory based on the archeological evidence.[6]

A POSSIBLE RECONCILIATION

Available evidence suggests that *Homo erectus* started in Africa but wandered far, and by about a million years ago could be found in such distant places as Europe, Southeast Asia, China,

and the Middle East. Each of the environments that character-
ized these regions was unique; in fact, each of these regions had
its own unique subregions. Some were hot and some were cold,
some were mountainous and others flat, some were sunny and
in others the weather was mostly cloudy. These and other factors determined whether a bipedal hominid was better off dark-
skinned or light, blond or brunette, stocky or lanky, and so forth.
As *H. erectus* settled down in each environmental zone, the
physical types best suited to it came to predominate, and over
thousands of generations the local population took on features
we now recognize as racial types in contemporary people.

Any other large mammal in such circumstances tends to
evolve, sooner or later, into separate species. This is what has
happened to various kinds of deer, bears, felines, and other
beasts we observe at the zoo. The first question we have to
answer, therefore, is, why did speciation not happen to *Homo
erectus*?

Perhaps there just wasn't time, in the million-plus years we
are considering. Other mammals have evolved into different
species in comparable periods, but something may have slowed
the process down for our forebears. One reason for the difference may have been that most other mammals have shorter
reproductive cycles and generation spans; a generation for a
deer is a lot less than for a human. Another—and this, as far as
I know, is pure speculation—is that we were more curious, more
travel-prone than most other species of mammals. There may
therefore have been appreciably greater interregional genetic
mixing, even before the arrival of *Homo sapiens*.

Perhaps, if you subscribe to the "Eve" theory, the question of
speciation became moot, because *Homo erectus* simply was
replaced. Perhaps *Homo sapiens*, emerging triumphantly from its
African cradle 130,000 years ago, simply killed all the *H. erectus*

cousins they ran across, clearing them out because they were competing for the same food and the same space. One hundred and thirty thousand years is enough to allow for a lot of walking, and a lot of migration, enough for our ancestors to reach all the extreme parts of the Old World. But does it allow enough time to allow for the development of the genetically inherited racial characteristics we observe in contemporary people?

There is a third possible explanation: *Homo sapiens* evolved relatively recently, in Africa, and spread out, as the geneticists think they have demonstrated. But as modern people dispersed, they interbred with the local populations of *H. erectus*. At least some of the offspring of these unions were "sapient" in their possession of brains that could conceptualize, and a capacity for language that gave them the verbal tools they needed for what now passes as human thought. Such hybrids were doubly advantaged in terms of their chances of surviving and passing on their genes in the specific environment in which they were born. They were the new models of the old winners, according to this explanation, and became the ancestors of modern racial groups.

From the biologists' point of view, this presents a difficulty: we define *Homo erectus* and *Homo sapiens* as different species, and the standard defining characteristic of a species is that all members can breed with each other but with no members of another species. But this is simply a matter of definition. The defining differences between *H. erectus* and *H. sapiens* are more temporal than morphological. If indeed *H. erectus* was the ancestor of modern men and women, and we have no better theory, then the first fully sapient individual must have been able to breed with somebody, or there would never have been a second. So it has to be incorrect to call *H. erectus* a separate species. We are dealing with a primitive form of our own *Homo sapiens*, and the only assumption you need to make to accept the third option is that representatives of the *H. erectus* lineage in places far from Africa had not yet evolved into entirely distinct species when the first *H. sapiens* arrived on the scene.

This third option would seem to offer a middle ground between the geneticists and the traditional archeologists.[7] It is an outline of a process, rather than an attempt to reconstruct prehistory. We are dealing with enormous time spans here, during which populations grew and diminished, flowed outward into new lands, and met and conquered other populations; or perhaps in some cases they met and mingled amicably. Who can know the details, at this remote distance?

ON MUTATION, AND BECOMING HUMAN

Biological evolution is incremental, as a normal rule. There are no great leaps forward; you do not have a generation of frogs producing a generation of lizards, or vice versa. But sometimes the minor adjustments in the genetic code that cause variation and lead to natural selection come in clusters, and even more rarely, such a cluster will have a synergy, a mutually reinforcing effect, that produces a powerful selective advantage. I believe something of this nature happened in Africa, perhaps about 130,000 years ago as the geneticists suggest, perhaps somewhat earlier. If so, then over a relatively short period of time, humanity as we know it was born.

The concept of several significant changes occurring at about the same time, and exerting a synergistic effect on each other, is consistent with accepted theory.[8] What, then, *are* the major components of the evolutionary breakthrough that produced our first fully human ancestors? The experts do not agree entirely here, but I would say that among these factors one should include:

- The development of a physical capacity for speech, involving changes in the position of the larynx and reduction in the size of the jaws and mouth.
- A substantial increase in the size of the brain. The capacity of the cranium expanded from about 1,000 cc to about 1,500, and the surface area doubled. The sections of the brain that enlarged the most were the ones that control the speech organs and the hands.

Together, these changes made possible both a capacity for abstract thought and a capability to communicate on an abstract level with other similarly endowed creatures. For the first time, an environment was established in which the creation, retention, and transmission of abstract concepts could flourish.

ON MIGRATION AND GENIC EXCHANGE

Our earliest thinking ancestors, by definition, didn't have much to go on by way of precedent as they gradually colonized a brave new world. But they were curious, and with their new capacity for abstract thought and speech, they had strengths like no other animal. Not even their cousins, the *H. erecti* that had spread out before them hundreds of thousands of years earlier, could begin to match their capacity for organization and their ability to adapt and innovate.

Our theory of human origins postulates that when the earliest sapient humans proliferated and expanded out into new territory, they sometimes interbred with indigenous populations of *H. erectus*. Such interbreeding is known in scientific circles as "genic exchange," and it could have taken two different forms.

The first and more comprehensible form of genic exchange is the mixing that occurs when a population moves into the territory of another. The two gene pools combine and produce a third one.

The second form of genic exchange is gene flow. This differs from the first form in that only the genes move. The people stand in place. They are like the individual drops of water bobbing up and down in the ocean. They mate with the people in the next tribe, perhaps as a matter of established custom, and the people next door also mate with people over on the other side, and so on, and given enough time a useful genetic trait can spread pretty far.

That sets the general scenario. I think it very likely that in the earliest days of our sapient ancestors' existence, their genes spread far and comparatively rapidly, both through direct interbreeding as a result of migration, and through gene flow. In due course, everyone around who qualified as *Homo* was *sapiens*; there were no longer any *erecti* left. The precise history of what happened to whom and when, who went where, during that early period of expansion, will probably never be known. But we shall probably know more eventually than we know now, if we keep on digging. And we shall. We are a narcissistic species and will never lose interest in how we began. Who knows, before very much longer we may even have resolved the conundrum of Neandertal man![9]

THE EVOLUTION OF HUMAN BEHAVIOR DURING THE PALEOLITHIC ERA

A growing number of scientists are exploring the roots of that elusive quality, human nature. They are probing into the murky gray area between psychology, anthropology, and biology, using an evolutionary lens. They ask, why do modern humans exhibit certain behavioral characteristics that seem to cut across cultures? What evolutionary purpose does, or did, such behavior serve? They conclude, for the most part, that these common behavioral features date back to the Paleolithic era—or in some cases, even earlier. It was in the Old Stone Age that our ancestors evolved what we now know as human nature. We are genetically equipped to cope with life in a hunter-gatherer milieu. The fact that we are, more or less successfully, now coping with life in a modern, overpopulated, technologically driven society is a triumph of cultural adaptation. Our genes are still adapted to the Paleolithic; they have yet to catch up with modern times. And given the slowness with which genetic evolution takes place, they never will—not in the foreseeable future.

This approach is unpopular with that influential school of anthropologists and sociologists who are committed almost as an act of faith to the proposition that genetics plays no appreciable role in determining the behavior of contemporary humans. Rather, they attribute all behavioral differences to culture. In the nature-nurture controversy, they are the all-out nurturists. But like the creationists, they are being forced by contemporary research to swallow an increasing body of evidence that points to a more even balance between genetics and environment as determinants of human behavioral patterns.

It seems there was an interplay between biological or genetic evolution and cultural evolution throughout the Paleolithic. The best description of how this worked that I have seen is by the distinguished Harvard biologist Dr. Edward O. Wilson:

> The swiftness of cultural evolution in historical times may seem by itself to imply that humanity has slipped its genetic instructions, or somehow suppressed them. But that is an illusion. The ancient genes and the epigenetic rules of behavior they ordain remain comfortably in place. For most of the evolutionary history of *Homo sapiens* and its antecedent species *Homo erectus*, *Homo habilis*, and *Homo ergaster*, cultural evolution was slow enough to remain tightly coupled to genetic evolution. Both culture and the genes underlying human nature were probably genetically fit throughout that time. For tens of thousands of years during the Pleistocene Epoch the evolution of artifacts remained nearly static, and presumably so did the social organization of the hunter-gatherer bands using them. There was time enough, as one millennium passed into another, for the genes and epigenetic rules to evolve in concert with culture. By Upper Paleolithic times, however, from about 40,000 to 10,000 years before the present, the tempo of cultural evolution quickened. During the ensuing Neolithic agricultural advance, the pace accelerated dramatically. According to the theory of population genetics, most of the change was far too fast to be tracked closely by genetic evolution. But there is no evidence that the Paleolithic genes simply disappeared during this "creative revolution." They stayed in place and continued to prescribe the foundational rules of human nature. If they could not keep up with culture, neither could culture expunge them. For better or worse they carried human nature into the chaos of modern history.[10]

THE ROOTS OF RACISM

The fossil record shows that *Homo erectus* had competitors, other hominid types which had evolved in parallel from apes. They were competing for much the same biological niche as *H. erectus*, and none of them survived. There are probably several reasons they became extinct, but I believe one of the main ones was that our own ancestors did not like the competition and went out of their way to eliminate them. As I shall argue in chapter 7, "On Aggression and Arms Races," there is evidence of a killer instinct imbedded in our human nature that goes back even farther than *H. erectus*, back to our chimpanzee-like ancestors five million years ago. When *H. erectus* began to roam far and wide, throughout all the regions of the Old World where we have found its traces, it must have encountered these competing hominid species and regarded them as hostile competitors and threats, to be fought and if possible exterminated.

Then came the next wave of human conquest, when *Homo sapiens* left the ancestral home base in Africa and replaced or absorbed regional populations of *H. erectus*. It is possible that in some cases the sapient newcomers were absorbed peacefully, but it would be stretching things to assume that the intermixing was always peaceful. It is more plausible to assume that the sapient visitors simply took over, using their superior intelligence and organizing abilities either to exterminate or to subjugate the resident population.

Think of the epics and sagas in human prehistory, the stories that have been long forgotten and can never be recovered, as our sapient ancestors walked all over the Old World, from Scandinavia to Indonesia and on to Australasia, meeting country cousins along the way, and either fighting it out with them for control of new territory, or settling down and mixing with them, or something in between! What a lot of human talent must have been developed and applied to the twin skills of war and diplomacy, even as in more modern times!

And then, later in prehistory, come the long sagas and epics of confrontations and collisions between different groups of fully sapient peoples, people who looked different and spoke in mutually unintelligible tongues. Here we can extrapolate backward in time from what we know about migrations and confrontations between different groups of people in early historic times; we can take the Old Testament of the Bible as a text. It is not unreasonable to assume that many of these confrontations were resolved on the battlefield rather than through diplomacy.

There has been a lot of negotiation and a lot of bloodshed along the road to the achievement of human society as we now know it. Much of it is prehistoric and will never be known; some of it is even prehuman. What started out as a conflict between species became a conflict between races, and then it merged further into a conflict between cultures. But the old roots remained. Whenever racial differences are present, they provide a powerful reinforcement to clashes between cultures.

There are still violent confrontations going on, and some of the worst involve racial differences. It takes a long time to get over habits we now view as bad, when they are so deeply ingrained, and played such an important part in fashioning us into the kinds of people we are. We have other bad habits we are trying to overcome, but racial hostility goes far, far back—which is why we are having such a hard time getting it under control.

As I write these words, I note a press report from central Africa, datelined Kinshasa: "An official radio station in the eastern town of Bunia on Aug. 8 urged Congolese to attack Tutsis, whom it described physically: 'Dear listeners! ... Open your eyes wide. Those of you who live along the road, jump on the people with long noses, who are tall and slim and want to dominate us.' "[11]

NOTES

1. I have used the definition provided by Richard Dawkins, Oxford don, zoologist, ethologist, author, and humanist, in *The Selfish Gene* (New York: Oxford University Press, 1989), p. 192.

2. The forest escaped being cut down and despoiled during the Second World War for a curious reason: Hermann Goering wanted it for his personal game park and hunting lodge after the Germans had won the war, and put it off limits for the Wehrmacht.

3. Many current books are available on this subject. For beginners, try the website "Human Prehistory: An Exhibition" at http://users.hol.gr/~dilos/prehis.htm.

4. The classic exposition of this theory is a book by my father: Carleton S. Coon, *The Origin of Races* (New York: Knopf, 1962). A more contemporary and rather different version can be found in Milford Wolpoff and Rachel Gaspari, *Race and Human Evolution: A Fatal Attraction* (New York: Simon & Schuster, 1997).

5. See Christopher Stringer and Robin McKie, *African Exodus: The Origins of Modern Humanity* (New York: Holt, 1998).

6. *Science News* 155 (February 6, 1999): 88.

7. Wolpoff and Gaspari, *Race and Human Evolution*. Wolpoff and Gaspari call their version of the multiple origins approach "multiregionalism." The explanation of human origins in this essay is based in part on "multiregionalism" and is broadly consistent with it.

8. This is what is sometimes known in expert circles as "saltation."

9. Fossil remains of Neandertal man are fairly abundant in Europe and the Middle East, but we still don't know: (a) whether Neandertals could speak; or (b) whether they were absorbed or exter-

minated. A thorough study of this issue is to be had in *The Neandertals*, by Eric Trinkaus and Pat Shipman (New York: Vintage Books, 1994). See also the readable, well-illustrated article in *National Geographic* 189, no. 1 (January 1996).

10. Edward O. Wilson, *Consilience* (New York: Vintage Books, 1999), p. 182.

11. James Rupert, *Washington Post*, October 1, 1998, p. A29.

CHAPTER 3

THE EVOLUTIONARY NATURE OF HUMAN THOUGHT

I t's time for a reality check. Can we distinguish between the "real world" out there and the mental techniques by which we humans relate to it? Can we distinguish between a "thing" in the material sense, and an abstraction?

The word "thing" has many meanings. I have consulted four dictionaries and each has at least a dozen definitions. To facilitate this discussion, I have chosen to restrict the meaning of the term as I use it here to the following: ". . . an object; anything which can be known or apprehended as having an existence in space or time as distinguished from anything which is purely an object of thought; as, goodness is not a *thing*, but an attribute of a *thing*."[1]

If I stub my toe on something, I feel pain and that tells me I have run into a "thing." The pain, however, is not a "thing" in the same sense. It is a series of electrical impulses flashing around parts of my nervous system. If I smell the roadside remains of a skunk, my mind will conjure up a mental image of a skunk, and while I may feel a flash of pity for the brute, I shall probably want to leave the vicinity quite promptly. The skunk and its smell are "things," but my mental reactions are not. If I get caught in the rain, the rain and the fact that I'm physically getting wet are "things," while my perception that I am getting rained on is not. And so on.

Until recently there was no analogue for the word "thing" as defined here that served as an equally general indicator of the various kinds of items that populate the world of the human mind. Perhaps the word "thought" comes closest. But is a song a "thought"? How about a technique for cooking a souffle, or a formula which allows you to convert kilometers to miles? Is there a word that signifies any and all thoughts, values, perceptions, patterns, techniques, strategies—a general term for mental "things"?

In *The Selfish Gene*, Richard Dawkins coined the word "meme" to fill this void.[2] It has caught on, at least in some circles. In Holland there is a *Journal of Memetic Studies*.[3] The term is used in different senses by different authorities, but it is no longer mere jargon. (If it were, I wouldn't introduce it here. I wouldn't anyway, except for the fact that I have found it a lot easier to discuss human culture when it is used.)

Perhaps we need to reexamine our definition of reality. There *is* a real world out there, consisting of things. But there's another world inside our minds, consisting of memes. We inhabit the biosphere, the world of "things," but we also live in our own world of thoughts and perceptions. Who is to say which of these worlds is real, and which is not? Which is more real, the acoustical experience of hearing a great musical work, or the paper on which the score is written? Which has proven to be more real throughout recorded history: the concept of God, or the structures in which people have worshiped Him?[4]

We all perceive the world of "things" through "memes": the values, memories, assumptions, and other mental constructs that determine the nature of our perceptions and how we shall respond. Equally, our personal neural network controls the conceptual inputs we receive from other people. Each of us, in other words, lives in two worlds at the same time: the physical world, and the world of ideas that is constantly flowing between us and around us within human society.

THE BRAVE NEW WORLD OF THE HUMAN MIND

Other animals employ memes. Some bird calls, for example, are learned rather than genetically programmed. And there are the hoots and whistles and other sounds of certain marine mammals. But what an impoverished world that must be compared to the vast new world opened up by the human capacity for speech and the capacities for abstract thought and memory that come with it! Just as earth came to provide just the right combination of environmental factors for biological life to evolve and flourish, so the evolution of a talking, thinking animal opened up a new world in which memetic life could take off and reveal its astonishing potential, for the first time in the life of our planet.

We like to anthropomorphize and tell each other stories about talking dogs and such like. When I was young I read the Dr. Dolittle books by Hugh Lofting. What a wonderful man the good doctor was, and what powers he gained by being able to talk fluently and conceptually to so many different animals and birds! And how stupid the rest of us were by comparison, who had never developed Dr. D's linguistic skills! It was fun to be able to fantasize along these lines—but then, it was fun to believe in Santa Claus, too.

Much later, I have been reading about the efforts of certain scholars to communicate with a few of the more intelligent species of animals, especially chimpanzees and dolphins. It's amazing what they have been able to do. By bypassing vocalization, using only objects and hand signals, one bright chimp developed a vocabulary of a couple of hundred words. Chimps in the wild also seem able to develop a variety of nonverbal behavioral patterns that are learned, not inherited.[5] Certain behavioral patterns have been observed in some, but not all, groups that have been studied, including techniques for cracking nuts, slapping tree branches to get attention, and clasping a comrade's arms overhead. Can we discern here the rudimentary beginnings of separate cultures?

But what is really amazing is that such feats amaze *us*. If that's the best our nearest relatives can do, there must be a great gulf that separates our mental processes from theirs. Recent scholarly studies are beginning to help us understand the nature of that gulf, and what it is about our own mental processes that are so special.[6] I shall attempt a synthesis here, recognizing that some authorities will consider it either inadequate or incorrect, given the current high level of controversy.

We think like other animals, but with a difference. The similarities stem from the fact that our brain doesn't "think" in words, but rather in patterns of neural activity; certain parts of the brain flash on and off, establishing patterns much the way the pixels on a television screen flash on and off, thereby establishing ever-changing patterns. When I smell a dead skunk on the side of the road, I do not immediately conjure up the word "skunk" in my mind; I flash on a pattern within my brain that tells me it is a skunk and not something else. When I am walking through the woods and spot a deer, I don't need the word to know that a deer is what I am looking at. The neural pattern the sight evokes in my brain tells me all I need to know. In exactly the same way, the deer looks at me and freezes, or else runs away. A pattern has just flashed on in that deer's mind that says: "Man!" The deer doesn't need the word to know what it has spotted. If it did, it wouldn't spot me, because it has no speech, no vocabulary, no word to express what it has seen.

When the deer and I spot each other, each of us associates what we see with memory. The deer remembers that what it sees is out of the ordinary and potentially life-threatening. It may remember the last hunting season and a close brush with death. If it is sure that it is a man it has spotted, it bounds away. If it is not sure, it may just freeze for about two minutes, to see if I move. If I do move, the deer's suspicion is verified and it flees. But if I stay absolutely still, then after two minutes its memory of man goes away; the neural pattern fades and is replaced by another. It resumes its foraging. If I move suddenly, the man-pattern is reactivated, more strongly this time, and the deer bounds off. But if I move slowly, the deer doesn't spook, at least for a while. It was sufficiently reassured by my nonmovement during those first two minutes, so that it can tolerate some movement on my part, at least for a little while.

Other animals have memory, but it only comes into play when stimulated by some event in the external tangible world of "things." For the deer I have described, the event was spotting me. But events need not be that specific, or alarming. I have a dog that loves to go for walks and comes to me every morning to ask that I take her out. In this case the "event" that triggers her request is the time of day and a daily routine she is familiar with. The point is that animals, except for man, are incapable of the kind of free-flowing, temporally unbound abstractions we take for granted when communicating with each other.

We can think in abstractions because we have language. It makes all the difference. Our brain has evolved into a larger size in large part because we need the extra capacity to produce the complex neural patterns that are associated with talking and listening, communicating with other humans. We use such patterns for the "memes" that exist in our social world as well as for the "things" that exist outside. With those memetic patterns, the sky's the limit. We are no longer restricted to thinking about what is happening around us, for our memes can take us back and forth in time, and out into space beyond anything we can see, hear, or smell. I can think of the word for deer, and even if there isn't a deer within a hundred miles, I can embark on a train of thought that leads by association to recollections of deer I have encountered, and to whatever knowledge I have stored in my memory about them generally.

MEMES AS AN EVOLVING FORM OF LIFE

Dawkins points out that memes, like living things, follow the basic principle cited earlier, namely that *all life evolves by the differential survival of replicating entities.*

A meme spreads by being copied from one individual's mind to another through a process known as "imitation."[7] The meme thereby achieves a replication analogous to what a biological thing achieves when it reproduces. When I tell someone a good story, the chances are the story will replicate itself. Every time the radiation theory of human origins is picked up and used in either the press or a scientific journal, that theory has replicated. When a song is popular, its success at replicating itself many times over is guaranteed. A meme that appears in print is replicated when it is read.

While living things compete in the biosphere, memes compete in the world of the mind with other memes for limited space in the particular niche they occupy. If that space were unlimited, all ideas, songs, and theories would be equally accessible and accepted. But none of these outcomes occur in the world of human thought, because human minds have only a finite capacity to absorb, retain, use, and disseminate memes. Each individual human has to decide which memes to accept and which to reject. Conscious thought is to a large degree devoted to just this.

We constantly filter out the vast majority of the memes that come our way. In deciding which ones to keep (remember and/or record) and which to discard (ignore or forget), we use our individual likes, prejudices, values, and other criteria. But we all agree on one basic criterion—we select only those memetic inputs that we think will be useful to us, or congenial, or both.

So the meme requires more than just an individual human brain for its existence. It may originate in a single mind, but from there on it operates in the context of a *group* of people who together decide whether it survives. That group can be as small as a family or as large as the present population of the world. Whatever its size and character, that group is the environment in which the meme lives, and frequently dies.

A caveat: the processes that determine how memes originate, spread, and die bear no intrinsic relation whatsoever to the processes that determine biological evolution through the transmission of genes. Memes evolve, as do genes, but through different mechanisms. Analogies can be misleading, and as between memes and genes, they usually are.

Having said that, I believe this concept—that memes can be considered another form of life because they follow the basic evolutionary principle of replication and selection—can provide us with powerful conceptual tools. If we are on target, we ought to be able to establish taxonomies for the creatures of the mind, roughly the way we have over the past several centuries established a classification system that includes all the biological life-forms we have found around us on the earth. Armed with this kind of conceptual framework, we should be in a better position than we are now to sort out relationships between different kinds of mental constructs. It should then become easier to adapt the evolutionary approach that scientists have used to explain life on our planet to analysis of the complex ideas that govern our social relations and indeed the entire mental universe we inhabit.

Ideas have lineages. The great philosophers never started from scratch; they built on, enlarged, and expanded ideas they picked up from existing authority. The same can be said for political systems and economic theories. Even such mundane ideas as the proper design for an automobile can be seen to have evolved over time from earlier models. If this is obvious, then it should be equally obvious that the mental baggage we carry around with us at present descends from the winners in the competitions between ideas that have been going on for a long time. That competition goes all the way back to the beginning, when our ancestors first developed a capacity for abstract thought.

NOTES

1. *Webster's New International Dictionary*, 2d ed., s.v. "thing."

2. Richard Dawkins, *The Selfish Gene* (New York: Oxford University Press, 1989), p. 192.

3. The website is http://www.cpm.mmu.ac.uk/jom-emit/.

4. This isn't, of course, a new concept. The idea of separate realities, nature and the world of the mind, goes back at least to Plato, who argued that the latter was the true "reality."

5. *Science News* (June 19, 1999): 388.

6. The literature on this subject is growing rapidly. Three books I can recommend are: Stephen Budiansky, *If A Lion Could Talk* (New York: Simon & Schuster, 1998); John McCrone, *The Ape that Spoke* (New York: Avon, 1991); and Steven Pinker, *The Language Instinct* (New York: W. Morrow and Co., 1994).

7. Susan Blackmore, *The Meme Machine* (Oxford: Oxford University Press, 1999), chap. 4.

CHAPTER 4

CULTURE

WHAT CULTURES ARE

The word "culture" has many meanings. For my purposes, I shall use the following definition: "the totality of socially transmitted behavior patterns, arts, beliefs, institutions, and all other products of human work and thought characteristic of a community or a population."[1]

The criteria by which cultures define themselves, and differentiate themselves from other cultures, vary a great deal. It's like cooking: you start with some basic ingredients and add a few condiments. The basic ingredients here are geography, ethnicity, language, religion, and history. The factors that divide cultures can consist of any combination of these elements, plus the "condiments" supplied by the local scene. In Morocco, the split between Berbers and Arabs is mostly linguistic. Ethnicity as such is a marginal factor at most. In Bosnia, the division between Serbs, Croats, and Muslims is almost entirely religious, as it is in Lebanon, where a population of ethnically homogeneous Arabs is divided among Sunnis, Shias, Christians, Druzes, and other sects. Kurds distinguish themselves from neighboring cultures, mainly Turks, Arabs, and Persians, on geographic, ethnic, and linguistic grounds. Within Afghanistan, the fault lines are mainly ethnic and linguistic. In India, the deep split is religious, between Hindus and Muslims, but the Hindu majority is split many ways, with the primary loyalty of the individual going to the subcaste in which he or she was born. In America, Germany, Japan, and other modern nation-states, group loyalties based on cultural differences still exist, but only as subsets; they have been subordinated to a relatively recent form of overarching group loyalty called "nationalism," sometimes called "patriotism."

A culturally defined group can be as small as a tribe in the Amazon basin, or as large as a nation-state. It can occupy a distinct area in space, or have its members share a territory with other culturally defined groups. It can be a vestigial survivor of a formerly more numerous and powerful community, or it can be expanding at the expense of neighboring groups. It can be a closed system, or wide open to new ideas from other cultures. There can be hierarchies of cultures, where subcultural units exist within a larger cultural group.

In short, the parameters of a culture can be as varied as the human condition itself. The only requirement is that the people who share it sense that they are different from people who do not belong to their group.

The distinction we established between "things" and "memes" is helpful here. As used in this book, a "culture" is a complex aggregate of memes shared by a group of people, which provides the individuals within that group with a sense of identity. These memes may be fairly static, or they may be changing. They may be identical in many ways to the elements that define neighboring social groups, but there will be enough differences so that the individuals within each group "feel" the difference. Indeed, it is much easier to describe such groups subjectively, from the viewpoint of the insider, than it is to stand back and provide a general, scientifically based portrayal. For the most important characteristic of a "culture" as I use the term here is the sense felt by the individual members of the group that they form a community, that they have shared interests, and that there are certain qualities that distinguish them from other people.

A caveat: while a culture is composed of memes, not all memes are building blocks of a culture. Cultural patterns have tended throughout history to be relatively stable, and to evolve only slowly, both in terms of their memetic elements and in terms of the population of individuals they include. There are many other kinds of memetic patterns floating around in people's minds, from the highly complex to the simple. Some of these patterns are universal, some are confined to a very small portion of a single group of people. But it is the memes that combine to create in the minds of men and women the particular phenomenon known as culture that concern us here.

When I talk about culture, I am discussing a way of describing groups of people that is very similar to what is popularly known as "ethnicity." Recently the world was shocked by reports of genocide and "ethnic cleansing" in Kosovo; before that it was Bosnia and Rwanda. Such conflicts don't necessarily involve ethnic groups as such; they involve collisions between groups distinguished not just by their ethnic origins but by their whole cultures. A sense of ethnic difference is one of several criteria by which cultures differ, but it is by no means the only distinction, and in some cases it isn't even a major factor at all.

As a diplomat, I explored a culture by getting inside it, by trying through reading, observation, and talking to people to gain some idea of how the people in the culture I was studying viewed society and the rest of the world. It was a subjective approach, not particularly scientific, but it brought home to me how central this attitude of "us vs. them" can be to any orderly understanding of contemporary human societies and how they got that way. Throughout human history and prehistory, culture has played a central role in determining how people organize their lives, philosophically and practically. If you want to know why someone behaves in a certain way, the first place to look is that person's culture. People stick with their "native culture" because they are proud of it, feel comfortable in it, and feel more comfortable dealing with other members of their own group than with outsiders. Emigration to another cultural zone involves a major psychological wrench and, as Americans know, it usually takes at least a generation to accomplish the metamorphosis we call "acculturation."

Let me digress for a personal anecdote. In the mid-1960s I was consul and principal officer at our very small American consulate in Tabriz, Iran. The consular corps was miniscule; there was a Turkish consul general, a French consul, and me; that was it. Protocol was usually relaxed, but occasionally some official event occurred which required the presence of the consular corps. We three consuls would drive up in our official vehicles, national flags flying, in order of rank, the Turk being first, as he was a consul general. When the affair ended, we would drive off in the same order.

I had two drivers on my staff, an Armenian named

Khotschig and a Turkic-speaking Iranian named Hosein. Khotschig was by far the cleverer of the two, and good company; Hosein was amiable but stolid. The first time I had to attend a protocol event, I took Khotschig. All was well when we drove up, but when it was time to leave, lo and behold, Khotschig was out front, ahead of the vehicle of my Turkish colleague, sailing me off in violation of protocol, to the annoyance of both my Turkish colleague and the Iranian authorities. I gave him hell, explaining the situation in detail. But the second time around, the same thing happened. This time he shamefacedly admitted that as an Armenian, he simply could not bear to let a Turk get ahead of him. It was like asking a dog not to bark at a cat. The Armenian folk-memory of the massacre of their people in Turkey was as vivid for him as it had been for his grandparents. From then on, I had Hosein drive me to protocol events.

Contemporary social scientists, for the most part, have viewed culture in a more detached way than I have, and not all would agree with me on its central role. But their research has clearly identified and parsed out most of the major differences that divide the cultural groups that exist on our planet today. And out of all this wealth of data, a clear pattern emerges.

Linguists, for example, have catalogued language and dialect differences all over the world in great detail. Similar research has occurred in the field of nonverbal communication, pioneered by the anthropologist Edward T. Hall, who demonstrated how in any given culture the purely verbal elements of interpersonal communication are backed up by a complex and culturally specific array of behavioral and other signals.[2]

Language and nonverbal behavior patterns are usually important elements of cultural differences. Much the same can be said for religion and for other major ways human behavior and interaction are governed. In the case of religion, communities develop their own sets of shared assumptions and practices. The assumptions have to do with beliefs, while the practices concern ritual and religiously prescribed rules of acceptable behavior. When communities sharing a common faith split and the parts become isolated from each other, doctrine and ritual follow suit and develop regional variations, just as languages develop dialects and eventually become separate tongues. Values and ethical systems evolve in a parallel manner and end up determining everything from definitions of truth and beauty to fashions in clothing.

AN EVOLUTIONARY REASON WHY CULTURES EVOLVE

All very good, there is general agreement as to the variety of cultures on the earth today. But how and why did they get that way?

Evolutionary theory provides simple and elegant answers to these questions. The following principles would seem to apply across a broad spectrum of cultures:

- A successful culture will grow. The size of its population will usually increase, while the division of labor within its ranks will become more complex. There is a simple explanation: When two cultures collide, it is usually the one with more people and a more elaborate division of labor that will prevail. For example, if the collision involves outright war, a large and well-organized army will almost always beat a smaller rabble. Competition between cultures, over the long run, thus favors the big and complicated over the small and simple.

- Cultures tend to intensify those factors that strengthen internal bonds. Moral codes, religious rituals, speech patterns, nonverbal behavioral patterns, and ways of dressing all become more tightly focused and more culture-specific over time. Again, there is a simple explanation: when two cultures collide that are fairly evenly balanced in terms of size and complexity, the one with the stronger internal bonds is likely to prevail. Mental patterns and practices that help members of a group distinguish themselves from outsiders are the glue that holds the community together. A passionate devotion to one's own group, and to the memes that distinguish it from other groups, is nothing more or less than the logical outcome of an evolutionary process. This principle helps explain why, over the long course of human history, so many people have been willing to die for their religion or for their tribe or nation. If you want to understand the root causes of the hostility between groups in the Balkans, or the Middle East, or Central Africa, or many other troubled parts of the world, this is as good a place to start as any.
- Technology as well as internal cohesion can increase the survivability of a culture. A large and complex cultural group is more likely to produce useful technological innovations than a small one, and it is more likely to contain individuals who will borrow useful innovations from outside.

CULTURES COMPETE IN MANY WAYS

We need to pause a moment at this point and consider what we mean when we say that one culture "prevails" over another. In a few cases, cultures collide and one exterminates the other.

Rome destroyed Carthage. Perhaps in the very early hunter-gatherer phase, this occurred fairly frequently—we don't know. During more recent periods, as far as we can tell, outright extermination has occurred only infrequently.

Somewhat less drastic would be warfare between two groups where the winners kill or enslave the male losers while keeping the females. Another pattern would be the forced migration of the losers, male and female, into new territory. If the cultures were somewhat related to each other, either of these outcomes would be more likely than total extermination. If the cultures were even more closely related, however, a war between them would more probably lead to some form of unification. The result might be an alliance, or an empire, or a single culturally homogeneous group.

Why do cultures collide? Usually there is a mixture of economic and resource issues, and often a territorial factor. Whatever the objective reasons for the hostility, the existence of intercultural differences exacerbates the problem and makes peaceful resolution of the dispute more difficult.

Not all cultural collisions are resolved violently. We can have shooting wars, but we can also have trade wars, and even soccer wars. Less bellicose forms of competition, particularly the trade or barter of goods and services between cultures, can benefit everybody in the short term as well as the longer run. Conspicuously successful societies can draw people from other groups to themselves, in ways that are more like osmosis than war. The United States is a prime example. It usually takes at least a generation for cultural assimilation to work, but taking the long view, this kind of osmosis can and does happen.

Peaceful resolution of collisions between cultures is all very well, and it is happening more frequently in modern times, but it runs counter to human nature. Since a culture, as I define the term, involves a sense of group loyalty, its members can and often do develop an equal but opposite sense of hostility toward a neighboring but different cultural group. This is particularly likely to happen when the sense of solidarity within the group is strong. Seen historically, almost everywhere we find a dreary repetition of the same scenario: two cultures are neighbors. One thing leads to another and there is a conflict. This creates a historical basis for further hostility, and intermittent warfare. It becomes a vicious circle, with the perception leading to the deed, which in turn fortifies the perception.

Everyone is aware of communal strife in the former Yugoslavia, of ethnic and other conflicts in Africa, and of strife in Afghanistan. I believe that all these situations fit readily into the pattern of competition between culturally defined groups. We who live in North America and in Western Europe don't suffer from this kind of strife, at least to the same degree, for a sense of national identity has taken over and has softened the edges of most of the subcultural differences that still exist. We should not, however, assume that the social environment we grew up in is standard for the world as a whole, and that conflicts in places like Central Africa are aberrations. If anything, the reverse is a truer statement of the general human condition, especially if one looks back down the long corridors of time that our ancestors have traversed. We "Westerners" are the true aberration, in that we have managed to break with the past and forge a new comity that submerges and controls the culture-based rivalries of our ancestors.

THE TEAM SPIRIT:
NURTURE OR NATURE?

Why do people behave this way? Why do so many people get so wrapped up in loyalty to their own group that they can, when provoked, go off and slaughter other people just because their victims belong to a different tribe or creed or nation? Were we all born that way? Is this an essential part of our human nature?

These are not easy questions. To answer them objectively we have to step back from the moral and ethical precepts we learned when we were first growing up in our own cultures. We have to think like observers, not participants.

A good way to start is to review what the behavioral scientists have learned about human nature. We have always been social animals. We acquired from our prehominid ancestors an instinct for banding together in groups, and that instinct not only survived but was strengthened because it conferred survival value. During Paleolithic times members of tribal-sized groups cooperated to ensure a regular food supply and share the kinds of knowledge and experience that helped them cope with adversities. There was no place for loners those days.

This social instinct provided the basis or launching pad for a singular efflorescence of culture as a means of providing group identity to larger groups. Such larger groups evolved inevitably, once agriculture and animal husbandry became widespread and militated the emergence of more complex social structures. Every distinctive feature of the cultures that began to arise in the earliest historic era was learned rather than passed on genetically, but the propensity to band together is part of our human nature.

Contemporary research suggests that the human mind is

programmed genetically to take just about any continuous spectrum of information that comes to it from the outside world and chop it into categories. Visible light, for example, is a gradual spectrum of frequencies before it hits the eye, but something in the brain sorts it out into colors before or while the mind "sees" it. Either that same genetic predisposition, or a closely related one, seems to be operating in the way each individual perceives the spectrum of people around him, running from close relatives through acquaintances all the way to complete strangers. Dr. Edward O. Wilson refers to "the dyadic instinct, the proneness to use two-part classifications in treating socially important arrays. Societies everywhere break people into in-group vs. out-group, child vs. adult, kin vs. non-kin . . . they fortify the boundaries of each division with taboo and ritual. . . ."[3]

This "dyadic instinct" helps explain why human society evolved in the direction of increasingly distinctive cultural units. Once launched on this trajectory, cultural collisions and the attendant need for loyalty within the cultural units can explain why individual cultures developed elaborate moral codes and apparently nonfunctional features like dietary prohibitions.[4]

In contemporary times, the instinct for distinguishing the in-group from the out-group operates with traditional force only for individuals who have been raised in monocultural environments. That instinct explains why Michel Husseini felt the "us vs. them" syndrome with such force and passion that it overrode his teacher-student relationship, his Christian ethic, and indeed his common humanity (chapter 1). In a multicultural environment, the "us vs. them" syndrome expends itself relatively harmlessly in activities like sports, business, and the politics of coalition building. But that same instinct, when it operates within a single cultural environment, can and often does become a monster.

The Husseini incident, and perhaps a hundred others I could cite, provide the basis on which I assert that at least some level of rivalry is endemic between culturally identified groups. I find that this principle explains a large amount of data in an economical fashion; it explains virtually everything I have observed in the Near East and South Asia, and is consistent with a great many events I have been hearing about in other parts of the world. It appears simplistic only in the more highly developed and rich regions, where complex issues have come to the fore that are not directly related to rivalries between communities. But that is the point. Humanity is changing. We are like a butterfly coming out of its cocoon. That cocoon is precisely what I am trying to describe when I discuss the principle of competition between cultures and its evolutionary impact.

Once the principle of endemic rivalry between culturally identified groups is recognized, much of human history as we know it can be explained as a working out of such rivalries over time and space. Once established, *Homo sapiens* didn't break into separate biological species, it divided on cultural lines, and evolution went into a higher gear. Now, after a hundred or so millennia of cultural competition, humanity is shifting gears again. This is a fun time to be alive, if a bit noisy.

CONCEPTUAL TRAPS

The concept that memes evolve is self-evident, or should be. However, most readers are likely to have more difficulty with certain concepts that flow from it: (a) cultures consist of relatively stable aggregates of memes, (b) cultures are themselves evolving, and (c) human society as a whole has evolved throughout most of its history largely because of competition between cultures. Part of the problem is that a lot of people are still confused as to what a meme really is, and even among "meme-ologists" there is considerable disagreement. But even if everybody accepted the definition I have proposed in the previous chapter, serious problems would remain.

For example, we are proposing that memes be considered another form of life because, as in genetically based evolution, memes follow the basic evolutionary principle of replication and selection. We cannot, however, carry the analogy to biological life very far beyond that initial point of similarity without getting into serious trouble. Memes, like living things, evolve and become specialized in response to the emergence of special environments, which they in turn influence, producing further change. Memes, like biological organisms, tend to combine and form increasingly complex aggregations. But the environments within which evolution takes place are completely different. Memes combine and recombine, specialize, flourish, and become extinct in ways and according to processes that can be very different from those that determine how living things evolve. They march to different drummers, on different roads. The only similarity is the fact that memes and living things are both on the march.

Many social scientists question whether evolution through cultural competition is the right paradigm through which to analyze the ways human societies have become more complex and sophisticated. They point out that in biological evolution there is no competition between species as such, there is simply an enhanced tendency toward survival for the individual that happens to carry the favored genetic pattern. Natural selection operates at the level of that individual, not the group as a whole. How then can we assert when dealing with memes not genes that the selection process takes place through the social group and not the individual human? Isn't there a basic flaw in the idea that social groups are subject to natural selection? Shouldn't we reject the whole idea of "group selection"?[5]

This approach is based on a false connection in the minds of the anthropologists, and indeed most of the other academics engaged in this controversy, between cultures and genes. There just isn't any direct connection between the way genes evolve, and the way cultures change over time. When cultures collide, leaving winners and losers, there need be no genetic trail left behind. There are no direct implications for the genetic makeup of the participants on either side. Cultures operate according to their own rules, which have nothing to do with the detailed processes that govern DNA composition, modification, and transmission.

I would urge observers of this scene to free up their thinking and take a larger, more inclusive view of how memetic evolution works. What evolves in biological evolution is a pattern of DNA carried by individuals. In memetic evolution there is nothing comparable to DNA as a single structural mold within which evolution occurs: there are different kinds of memes, and different kinds of aggregates of memes, that evolve along different paths. Cultures constitute just one of many categories of mental aggregates, or "memeplexes" to use Susan Blackmore's term.[6] However, compared to most other memeplexes, cultures are unusually durable. They resemble DNA, therefore, in that both are patterns of information that evolve through a process of selection over relatively protracted periods of time. But they differ completely in the nature of the entity that contains the pattern and transmits it. For DNA that entity is the individual, while for a culture, it is the group as a whole.

Serbs and Albanian Kosovars have been locked in mortal conflict recently. The Serbs *as a community* were naturally selecting the Albanians—selecting them out, that is—until a larger and more complex society (NATO) intervened and put a stop to it. Why the conflict? Must we insist that the explanation lies in a reductionist attempt to analyze each individual's motives? Is there no general pattern to explain the hostility? If there is, it is based on history and geography and ethnicity and language and religion—all the ingredients I cited as providing groups with a sense of cultural identity. Surely this is a classic contemporary example of a collision between cultures. The cultural explanation is simple, obvious, and sensible. In my opinion, no others need apply.

Perhaps the problem can be resolved by a simple change in terminology. Let us reserve the phrase "natural selection" for the biological process of selection which operates primarily through the genes of living creatures, and use the parallel phrase "cultural selection" for the kind of memetic or social evolutionary process we are primarily concerned with here.

There's another problem with our effort to explain human social evolution in memetic and cultural terms. Some scholars object that this approach simply uses fancy new terminology to repeat what the world's philosophers and historians and other theorists have been saying all along about humanity and human nature. Perhaps they are right, to some extent. Certainly historians like Arnold Toynbee have had a lot to say about how whole societies rose and fell over time. Many philosophers have dealt with the evolution of ideas. Relatively mundane time lines like the ones for automobile or aircraft evolution have been described in great detail. So what's new? Are we adding nothing more to the store of human understanding than some fancy new jargon?

What is new is an overarching conceptual framework within which all these relatively familiar approaches can be joined together. What will be new, once we have a generally accepted way of thinking about memes and the cultures they form, is a fresh opportunity to see how they fit together, and to look for common features. At least that is what I envision, after we have parsed out how memetic evolution works more fully than we have so far.

There is a third objection, which is surprisingly widespread even though it is founded not on reason but on emotion. It is a visceral reaction to anything that bears even a superficial resemblance to that politically incorrect set of beliefs lumped under the term "Social Darwinism." This is enough of a red flag, and so off-putting to many readers, that I have devoted the next chapter to it. I hope it will persuade those readers who may be infected with the "anti-social-darwinist" meme that what I am proposing is totally different from the theories that inspired the antisocialism of the robber barons or the foul racism of the Nazis.

To sum up: the concept that our thoughts evolve is, or should be, self-evident. The further concept that thoughts combine to form cultures, and that cultures evolve through natural selection, is not nearly as evident, nor is it as widely accepted. But if the idea is handled carefully, bearing the above caveats in mind, it can contribute new perspectives to our understanding of how humanity arrived at its present complex condition.

NOTES

1. *The New Heritage Dictionary*, 2d College ed., s.v. "culture."

2. Edward T. Hall, *The Silent Language* (Garden City, N.Y.: Doubleday, Anchor Press, 1959); idem, *The Hidden Dimension* (Garden City, N.Y.: Doubleday, Anchor Press, 1966); idem, *Beyond Culture* (Garden

City, N.Y.: Doubleday, Anchor Press, 1976); *The Dance of Life: The Other Dimension of Time* (Garden City, N.Y.: Doubleday, Anchor Press, 1983); Edward T. Hall and Mildred Reed Hall, *Hidden Differences: Doing Business with the Japanese* (Garden City, N.Y.: Doubleday, Anchor Press, 1987); idem, *Understanding Cultural Differences* (Yarmouth, Me.: Intercultural Press, 1990).

3. Edward O. Wilson, *Consilience* (New York: Vintage Books, 1999), p. 182.

4. Robert A. Hinde, *Why Gods Persist* (London: Routledge, 1999), pp. 180–82.

5. George C. Williams, *Adaptation and Natural Selection: A Critique of Some Current Evolutionary Thought*, rev. ed. (Princeton, N.J.: Princeton University Press, 1996). Williams' scholarly analysis concludes that group selection is hardly ever a valid explanation for adaptive change in the biological world; rather, such change can almost always be explained more parsimoniously and correctly as the end result of adaptation on the part of the individuals who comprise the group.

6. Susan Blackmore, *The Meme Machine* (New York: Oxford University Press, 1999), p. 19.

CHAPTER 5

SOCIAL DARWINISM

I t was probably inevitable that when Charles Darwin's theories first burst on the scene, confusion would result. It was not inevitable that the confusion would last as long as it has. But regrettably, it is still with us.

Social Darwinism arose in the late nineteenth and early twentieth centuries. Various authorities took Darwin's theory of natural selection, which was originally intended to apply only to selection through genetic variability, and applied it in a crude fashion to selection between human groups differentiated by culture. As a guide not only to history, but to current policy, the notion spread that natural selection among humans, as among animals in a state of nature, required that the strong survive and the weak perish. The "law of tooth and fang" was elevated to a moral principle.

A school of thought led by Herbert Spencer, an influential contemporary of Darwin's, held that some people were naturally superior to others, and that the perfection of the species required that the inferior ones bite the dust, leaving the future of humanity to their betters. This theory merged conveniently with aspects of nineteenth-century capitalism to justify economic policies sacrificing social welfare in favor of rampant capitalism and the rich getting ever richer. Traces of that thinking persist in one form or another to this day.

Another version of "Social Darwinism" misapplied ongoing studies of the individual races of humankind to claim that certain racial groups were superior. This line of thinking provided a pseudo-intellectual underpinning to the racist doctrines of the Nazis and thereby contributed to the Holocaust.[1]

These misapplications of evolutionary theory have made it difficult for contemporary observers to think objectively about competition between culturally identified groups and how that competition has affected the course of human evolution since the dawn of history. One social scientist has noted, for example, that "there is as yet no generally accepted evolutionary explanation for human social complexity. . . ."[2] The paper goes on to postulate that "the use of culture to erect symbolic barriers between groups can account for ethnocentrically limited altruism that underpins social organization."

There is a gap in contemporary thinking about human evolution. The evolutionary psychologists have examined our Paleolithic ancestors from a Darwinian point of view; meanwhile, they and other scientists have been exploring the nature of human nature as it exists today. The period in between has been left to the historians, and while they have done a great deal of competent research, it has seldom been inspired by an evolutionary perspective. It has simply not been fashionable to analyze human civilization using Darwinian conceptual tools—except for the Social Darwinists themselves. The Social Darwinists may be a spent force, but a substantial cadre of high-minded intellectuals, liberals, and anti-Nazis who ought to be taking an evolutionary look at human history are still too busy reacting against what they see as forces of bigotry, racism, and oppression to take on the job. A contemporary Darwinian look at history has, in short, been the victim of guilt by association.[3]

I do not wish to denigrate the efforts of thousands of competent historians, economists, and political scientists, among others, who have labored with various degrees of success to interpret and explain various dimensions of the contemporary world and its roots. The concepts I advance here are intended to supplement existing theory, not supplant it. I do believe that a visceral distrust of anything smacking of "Social Darwinism" has been critically important in obscuring the true nature of how our species has evolved and is still evolving. I hope that this book will demonstrate that a lot of things become clearer when we look at human history through an evolutionary lens, and accept without revulsion the principle that much of that history has been structured around the principle of competition between culturally differentiated groups.

NOTES

1. See Pat Shipman, *The Evolution of Racism* (New York: Simon & Schuster, 1994).

2. Peter J. Richerson and Robert Boyd, "The Evolution of Human Ultra-sociality," in *Indoctrinability, Ideology, and Warfare: Evolutionary Perspectives*, ed. I. Eibl-Eibisfeldt and F. Salter (New York: Berghahn Books, 1998), pp. 71–95.

3. For an example of how even a highly respected contemporary evolutionary thinker remains influenced by this history, see Stephen Jay Gould, "A Tale of Two Worksites," *Natural History* (October 1997).

CHAPTER 6

THE FIVE LEVELS
OF ALTRUISM

WHY ALTRUISM?

It had been snowing fairly heavily out here where I live in the Blue Ridge foothills. The roads were being plowed but people's driveways were for the most part blocked. If we had all been in Minnesota no one would have noticed, but here the problem was unusual. My sister-in-law called: could I bring my tractor over and plow out her driveway? Of course, I say, and I did. A bit of a nuisance, and of course it would have been different if a total stranger had asked me; but then, a stranger probably wouldn't have approached me in the first place. Joyce is family, and her husband would do the same for us if he hadn't been away.

Why do I feel this way? Because I have a strong sense of altruism toward family. I also feel altruistic toward other members of this fairly small rural county, especially the ones I know. But less so than for family. I feel very little altruism toward the strangers I meet in the big city, even though we are all citizens of the United States.

I've previously discussed the difficulty of defining a culturally identified social group, and concluded that the only litmus test that works generally is the sense of "us-vs.-them" that the in-group feels toward outsiders. Another way of expressing essentially the same idea is to define the group in terms of altruism. People within an in-group feel more altruistic toward other members of the group than they do toward outsiders. They are more inclined to trust another insider, for a wide variety of reasons. Within most groups, people speak the same language, and usually the same dialect. They dress the same way, and behave similarly, making it more likely that they share the same values. The fact that they are together in the same group makes it less likely that anyone will misuse the trust of the others; for one thing, any such betrayal will be more quickly apprehended and is more likely to be punished. People are, in short, more comfortable, more relaxed, and happier dealing with each other than with outsiders. When some crisis arises, they know which team they are on. It is a good feeling to belong to a culturally defined group. Social animals that we all are, it is the very stuff of life.

Social scientists have studied many aspects of the phenomenon known as altruism, until by now something that seems a simple concept to the amateur has turned into a labyrinth of learned discussion and debate. Matt Ridley's recent book, *The Origins of Virtue*,[1] is a readable effort to parse this debate out. For readers interested in game theory, and probing deeply into whatever it is in the human psyche that makes people behave altruistically, Ridley has much to offer. I won't try to repeat his argument, however; I'll try to keep my rendering of this abstruse issue as simple as I can. And to that end, I propose a simple fivefold classification for the levels of altruism that I see around me. It isn't perfect, for no such attempt to categorize pieces of a continuum ever is; but it works reasonably well.

THE FIVE STAGES OF ALTRUISM

The first level of altruism is simply an expression of the "selfish gene" principle[2] applied to other members of a genetically related family. That principle, which says that every biological organism operates under the primordial need to replicate its own genetic material, is not confined to humans, or even to primates. Among bees and ants, workers frequently sacrifice their own lives to protect the queen, who is the exclusive guardian of the group's genetic message. With mammals, a mother will protect her offspring, since the preservation of her own genetic message, as represented by her offspring, is supremely important to her genetically decreed sense of purpose.

With chimpanzees, gorillas, and humans, this level of altruism becomes somewhat more complex. In some circumstances, individuals will give up food, take sides, even sacrifice their lives for their siblings. The essential criterion is that the sacrifice should enhance the odds that the individual's own genetic message will be passed on to future generations, given the fact that the siblings share much of that genetic message. The chimp will be less likely to make similar sacrifices if the other individuals are less closely related.

The second level of altruism is based on cooperation between individuals that are not closely related genetically. It must have originated in small hunter-gatherer groups where everyone knew everyone else well. We can find this level with chimpanzees; they tend to live in bands that may include upward of thirty or forty individuals, who cooperate closely in such matters as food gathering, grooming, and sex, even though not every individual is directly related to every other one. Since the "selfish gene" principle cannot by itself ensure cooperation in a group this large, another principle is at work, that of "reciprocal altruism." This can be seen as the earliest beginning of the Golden Rule, the "do unto thy neighbor as you would have him do unto you" principle. It is directly and demonstrably utilitarian as long as every member of the band knows every other member reasonably well. You do your neighbor a favor knowing that he or she will remember and will reciprocate later on with another favor, perhaps of a different kind. Individuals who are insufficiently generous with their favors, or with repaying the favors of others, are recognized and identified, and other members of the group don't treat them very well.

The second level of altruism is, unlike the first, primarily human. Instances of reciprocal altruism have been observed among dolphins, chimpanzees, and other primates, but they are primitive by comparison with what humans achieved even relatively early in the prehistory of our species.[3] For these other animals, reciprocal altruism constitutes a kind of rare culmination, an apogee of social complexity; for our ancestors, it was just a beginning, a gateway to new and increasingly complex social orders. Our capacity for speech, and constructing a complex world of memes among ourselves, made all the difference.

Reciprocal altruism in a small human group enhances the whole band's chances of survival against the vagaries of a hostile environment, and in competition with other bands. But when there *is* competition from other bands, as we noted earlier, cultural selection operates in favor of increasing the size of the group. Over many generations what might start as a few small bands, of perhaps twenty or thirty individuals each, might coalesce into a larger tribe including perhaps a hundred or a hundred and fifty members. Individuals might still retain a primary loyalty to their immediate kin, and a secondary loyalty to the descendants of the original band, but there would be another, larger loyalty superimposed, to the other members of the tribe as a whole. In peaceful times there might be internal squabbles but when faced by an external threat the whole group would pull together. The same might hold true when hunts took place that required the cooperative effort of more hunters than a small band could muster.

When a tribe is small, little larger than an extended family, it is too small a breeding unit to provide the genetic diversity a healthy population needs. So two such bands might get in the habit of exchanging spouses, and develop close relations. Soon a pattern might be established of alliances between bands which, depending on circumstances, could lead to the formation of tribes, and even confederations of tribes. Whether such consolidation was caused mainly by intermarriage, by external threats, or by the need for cooperation in other matters, a high degree of cultural uniformity would soon evolve and enhance internal solidarity. At least that is the way we might describe it; seen from the inside, everyone would more or less share the "commonsense" view that each individual was a member of the team, because he or she "belonged" there, and behaved "properly," unlike outsiders.

This pattern of a gradual increase in the size and complexity of culturally defined units proceeded very slowly during the Paleolithic era. Tribal-sized units, small enough so that everybody recognized everybody else on sight, were probably the norm except in particularly favorable environments, where enough food was available to support a relatively dense population even at pre-agricultural levels of technology. It was a long period of incubation, perhaps a thousand or more generations, and during it was forged what we now popularly recognize as "human nature."

One notable feature of "human nature" is the way the conflict between selfishness (the "selfish gene" principle) and altruism led to increasingly complex behavior. The selfish gene leads the individual to strive for status, since high status in most primate communities, including humans, tends to improve reproductive opportunities. This means competition, frequently of a zero-sum nature, with other individuals within the group. It inspires a "do in your neighbor and get ahead" attitude, leading to actions that tend to disrupt the tribal solidarity inspired by reciprocal altruism. In most individuals these two principles, selfishness and altruism, coexist in uneasy equilibrium. There is a kind of separation-of-powers principle at work here, with each principle acting as a check and a moderator on the other. When an individual is perceived to be acting in self-serving ways that hurt others excessively, he is beaten up, cast out of the tribe, or branded a sociopath and jailed, depending on the society concerned. So the ambitious, gene-driven individual usually seeks to advance his selfish interests in ways that are not perceived as unduly antisocial. Herein lies the basis for much human behavior, including hypocrisy, political expediency, and cynicism.

Perhaps equally important was the development of "work-arounds"[4] to resolve problems *within* the individual when behavior mandated by a higher level of altruism conflicted with the more "instinctive" behavior mandated at a lower level. As a functioning adult male your first and most important instinct is to provide food for your own immediate family. Perhaps the surest way to accomplish this is to go after rabbits and other small game. But the gang wants you to go out and hunt mammoths. You risk serious injury or death, you probably won't get anything yourself, and even if you do you have to share it with the whole group. (Your family couldn't eat it all by itself anyway.) And yet, mammoth hunting in certain environments, and at certain technological and social levels, works. (According to Ridley,[5] human hunters in the Paleolithic exterminated the mammoths much as the whites and the plains Indians almost exterminated the bison more recently.) What is the "work-around" that makes the mammoth hunter go hunt mammoths instead of rabbits? It is a culturally imposed sense that a certain behavior pattern is the "right thing" to do even though it is counterinstinctive. Culture cuts in here, as in many other situations, as an essential rule-maker and enforcer that mediates between conflicting patterns of behavior and makes possible the evolution of more complex societies and more efficient ways of coping with the environment.

The third level of altruism began to take shape when a few tribal units in particularly favored places expanded in size and complexity to the point where it was no longer possible that everybody within the unit knew everybody else. During the Paleolithic era this rarely happened. In most cases when the environment supported substantial populations, early hunter-gatherer societies would grow in numbers, split into subtribes, and expand their territory—a pattern observable with chimpanzees and other primates as well. When geographic expansion led to overlapping with some other tribe, conflict usually followed. The winners would take over the best of the contested land, and either absorb or expel the losers.

The most important exceptions to this pattern were certain areas, notably in the Near East, which particularly favored the breakthrough from the hunter-gather way of life to agriculture-based societies. As Jared Diamond has pointed out,[6] the Near East, and to a lesser degree regions such as China and parts of the New World, had at that time assemblages of wild grasses and other food plants, and animals suitable for domestication, that made such a transition possible. This breakthrough, wherever it occurred, led to the growth of relatively dense populations, which at first continued to be organized as large tribal-sized units.

As long as there was room for tribal-sized losers to move into empty land within these favored areas, the old pattern prevailed. But once the technical breakthroughs of agriculture and animal husbandry had been achieved, population rose dramatically and the good land filled up. Conflict continued on the tribal level, but there was no place for the losers to go except the adjoining desert, which was usually little better than dying in battle. Since the losers could no longer be expelled, they had to be either exterminated or absorbed. Humanity faced a new situation, involving a whole new constellation of issues and challenges, and perforce began a painful transition. Enter city-states, and the dawn of history as we know it. Kingdoms and empires followed.[7]

At that point altruism split along horizontal lines, as class distinctions arose between peasants on the one hand, and ruling warrior/priest coalitions on the other. The critical factor here was the enlargement of the sociopolitical unit beyond the stage where almost everyone could recognize almost everyone else. There is a threshold here that still applies today. A good manager decentralizes, because the average modern employee works best in a team environment, the team being as small as an old-fashioned tribe, or smaller. Many coaches, military leaders, and other managers understand this principle and capitalize on it. At any rate, when the city-states grew past this threshold, they evolved in a way analogous to the evolution of a one-celled creature to a multicellular one. Peasants at the village level plodded on with about the same tribal-sized loyalties as before. The new superstructure of rulers formed their own peer groups with their own group loyalties.

This enlargement of political and economic units required the extension of the principle of altruism to larger culturally united groups. Since it was no longer possible for everybody in the group to have at least a passing familiarity with everybody else, other forms of group bonding became essential. A more elaborate hierarchy of cultural standards was required to justify and enforce the maintenance of a new kind of social order, distinguishing between rulers and peasants. Conflict between culturally defined units continued, and made strong internal cultural bonds more necessary than ever to ensure the group's survival.

The result was an efflorescence of culture, in terms of its variety and pervasiveness. This whole epoch, from late in the Neolithic era until the dawn of the nation-state, can be considered the heyday of cultures; it was during this period that they played a dominant role in the evolution of ever more complex social units. Religion played an increasingly central role in many parts of the world. One tribe, to take a familiar example, might proliferate into twelve, but remain united by common observance of certain rituals and by common belief in an ancestral tribal god. Members of the new, larger units could identify other members of their group by appearance or dress or language or faith, even if they didn't already know them.

Third-level societies have declined in relative importance during the past several centuries, but they haven't yet disappeared. Some of them still are growing, and intensifying their internal bonds. It is this third level of altruism that holds together the warring factions that were recently fighting their neighbors in Bosnia, Lebanon, Burundi, and Chechnya. The hope of humanity for several millennia, they are now fast becoming its curse.

I have spent so many years in the Middle East and South Asia that it seems perfectly natural to me that society should be organized on this kind of a multicellular basis, with the individual's sense of altruism existing hierarchically on three ascending levels: kin, tribe (or village), and ethnic-linguistic-confessional community. The average Arab or South Asian is just as competent as anyone else in a multicultural environment, but as long as he is inside his native community, he makes a poor bureaucrat by Western standards. Why? Because when someone from his own group asks a favor, it must and will be granted. Institutional loyalties don't work if they run counter to traditional loyalties to clan or religious confession or ethnic group.

The Ottoman Empire, which ruled much of the Middle East from its capital in Istanbul for several centuries up to the First World War, was actually organized on this basis. Under the so-called millet system, each community in places like Syria and Iraq lived in its own quarter, had its own civil courts, and generally kept to itself, with the central government's interference restricted to taxation and defense. This system worked rather better than many of the more "modern" regimes that replaced it after the First World War.

There are many examples of third-level altruism and the cultural cohesiveness it spawns. A lot of them are in the Middle East, where a mosaic of culturally distinct peoples are mixed up geographically in an uneasy equilibrium. But even in the United States, traces are evident almost everywhere you look. Koreans have gravitated to small groceries, a South Asian subcaste is managing many of our motels, and one taxi firm in the nation's capital employs only Ethiopians while another employs only Sikhs. Language is a factor here, but there is more to it than that; and anyway, language is part of the cultural distinctiveness we are observing, isn't it?

While this third level of altruism can still be found almost everywhere, in the United States it has been submerged by the homogenizing impact of a national culture fortified by easy travel and instant communications. But it has not surrendered that easily elsewhere. Lebanon is an extreme example of what can happen when a new system takes over that expects the individual to be as loyal to the nation as to his own religious community. *That* kind of loyalty requires the evolution of a new level of altruism.

The fourth level of altruism, usually referred to as "nationalism," and sometimes labeled "patriotism," is associated with the modern nation-state. It is difficult to pin down a specific time and place when it first became an important thread in the fabric of human social evolution. Within the last couple of centuries, however, the nation-state has become the dominant form of political organization, and the most successful states have been the ones that could count on the loyalty of their citizens.

Nationalism took different forms in Europe and the United States. Well ahead of global trends, the United States began a century and a half ago to become a multiethnic, secular society. In Europe, nationalism was still, until quite recently, based on popular perceptions of ethnic and linguistic homogeneity. The Europeans are now catching up, as they strive to assimilate waves of immigrants, and as they move toward first economic and then political unity.

There is a distinction between nationalism and patriotism. Nationalism is competitive and often implies denigration of other countries as well as praise for one's own. Nationalism ran amok in the first half of the twentieth century and provided the psychological basis for two of the bloodiest wars in human history. Patriotism is simply love for one's country. It is a gentler form of altruism; it allows not only for pride in country but for tolerance elsewhere.

The fifth level of altruism is what I call "pan-humanism." It develops when an individual comes to believe that many millions of people, of varying creeds and colors, are all on his or her team. That individual can then internalize the concept that all humans are part of the same great experiment, and the Golden Rule applies to everyone.

ALTRUISM'S PRESENT AND FUTURE: NATIONALISM AND THE GLOBAL VILLAGE

I recognize that most Americans are still satisfied with old-fashioned loyalty to the United States and are uncomfortable, even hostile, to the idea that we owe everyone else in the world anything at all. But times are changing. The humanitarian instinct is, in modern times, becoming an expression of concern for all humanity and is a powerful influence on public policy.

The good news is that in terms of altruism, our species has demonstrated the will and the ability to adapt to changing circumstances in a fundamental way, not once but several times, if you accept the explanation proposed here. Given that record, I believe it is reasonable to assume that eventually humanity as a whole will once more respond to the challenge of the times, and achieve level five.

The bad news is that a very large number of the people on the planet right now haven't even achieved level four. We can ignore the ones still mired in the first two levels, kinship and tribe, for there are so few of them left. But that third level remains troublesome and probably will become even more so as population growth adds to present stresses in many of the poorer parts of the world. There are still far too many people who can be brought to believe that their god authorizes them to murder unbelievers. Or that their current misery can be attributed to a neighboring ethnic or linguistic group and can be alleviated by trying to kill them or drive them out.

Furthermore, we still have problems with some of our own number on level four. I refer not only to those who believe that war between fully developed nation-states is still a viable option. I also refer to those adherents of old-fashioned capitalism whose devotion to the bottom line leads them to permanently impoverish our common planetary support system.

But there is more good news. Humanism in the modern, universalist sense is an established movement, not yet on a par with the old gods in terms of numbers of followers, but triumphant in the battle of ideas. It forms ready and increasingly effective coalitions with environmentalist and other movements. World opinion is becoming a force that matters. Recently it helped bring an end to apartheid in South Africa. Amnesty International is a thorn in the side of repressive regimes all over the world. The Internet is bringing people from many areas together in pursuit of common interests. The poetry of global altruism infuses the music people are listening to. There is a sea change in attitudes under way, it is generational, and it is happening now.

Perhaps the best news of all is the message that evolutionary psychologists and other social scientists have validated: there is indeed such a thing as a basic human nature (chapter 2). Despite all our manifest differences, all people share the same basic mental programming. There is no evidence that any race, or any cultural or political group, has more or fewer of our ancestral instincts than anyone else. If some of us have made it out of level three, and even into level five, there is no genetic, biologically ordained reason the rest of us can't, too. People may use their mental assets differently, but we all begin at the same starting line.

This is a powerful building block for the pan-humanist view.

NOTES

1. Matt Ridley, *The Origins of Virtue* (New York: Penguin, 1996). Ridley is an English zoologist and science writer.

2. Richard Dawkins, *The Selfish Gene* (New York: Oxford University Press, 1989).

3. Ridley, *The Origins of Virtue*, pp. 157 ff.

4. Peter J. Richerson and Robert Boyd, "Complex Societies: The Evolutionary Origins of a Crude Superorganism," in *Human Nature* 10 (1999): 253–89.

5. Ridley, *The Origins of Virtue*, p. 107.

6. Dr. Jared Diamond, *Guns, Germs, and Steel* (New York: W. W. Norton, 1997). Dr Diamond is a professor of physiology at UCLA and a prolific writer of articles and books concerning evolutionary biology and biogeography.

7. The image of the surrounding desert applies more to the Middle East, i.e., the valleys of the Nile and the Tigris-Euphrates, than to other areas where agriculture may have evolved separately. It is an evocative image, in its suggestion that perhaps we may face a similar situation today on a global scale. (See chapter 16.)

CHAPTER 7

ON AGGRESSION AND ARMS RACES

I was visiting the site of the famous battle of Jericho, the biblical city outside Jerusalem. The year was 1954 and the site was being excavated by a large team under the direction of the distinguished British archaeologist Dame Kathleen Kenyon. Since my father was along, Dame Kenyon herself guided us around the dig. I remember going down an incredible distance, considering that every twenty feet or so of altitude change signified going back perhaps a millennium in time. At the lowest level so far excavated was the floor of a Neolithic house, with portions of a human skull and shoulder bone protruding. Archeologists with camel's-hair brushes and dental tools were carefully picking away at the surrounding debris. We watched for a couple of minutes and then continued our tour.

We returned a couple of hours later, to find that the team had revealed more of the skeletal material; now one could see down to the rib cage. The back portion of a flint spearhead, perhaps four inches in length and beautifully worked, stuck out between two of the ribs. There it was: eight or ten thousand years ago, somebody had bought the farm, most likely in a local war. He died in battle and when the survivors came back to reconstruct the village, they just built it right over him. Maybe the old village he had either been attacking or defending had been reduced to rubble and they didn't even know he was there.

It occurred to me then that you can be made just as dead by a flint-tipped spear as by an atom bomb. Our ancestors have been at this killing business for a long time.

Intertribal feuding is usually a matter of one thing leading to another; the stakes go up, and soon raiding parties exact their toll; then the eye-for-an-eye principle takes over. My father's first novel, *Flesh of the Wild Ox*,[1] graphically describes the dynamics of such a situation from the point of view of the participants, a quarrelsome lot of Berbers in the steep northern hills of Morocco known as the Rif. A Riffian tribe, the Ulad abd el-Mumen, gets crosswise with neighbors and someone gets killed; then someone on the other side gets a bullet through his ribs, and the party takes off. Mayhem follows, and ultimately the survivors of the Ulad abd el-Mumen are banished from the Rif mountains entirely. (This is a true account of events that occurred in the late nineteenth and early twentieth centuries, though my father wrote it up as fiction.)

Much the same process applies when warfare takes place on a grander scale. For example, take the Himalayan province of Kashmir, contested between India and Pakistan. In 1965, what started as a minor skirmish along the cease-fire line in that province rapidly escalated through a series of increasingly serious moves and countermoves into a full-scale war between India and Pakistan. Human history is full of such episodes. A little thing happens, there is retaliation, tension builds up, and pretty soon entire tribes or nations are killing each other.

ORIGINS OF HUMAN BELLICOSITY

There are grounds for believing that the habit of intertribal warfare goes way back, beyond the first humans, beyond the first hominids, to the ancestral primate from which both modern chimpanzees and modern humans are descended.[2] The evidence is based on recent studies of how modern chimpanzees behave in their natural habitat. One such study reports in chilling detail the activities of chimpanzees living in an undisturbed state in central Africa. Like wild chimps that have been observed elsewhere, these animals travel in bands, numbering a couple of dozen or so. Male chimps within a band periodically form troops of about four mature individuals in their prime who patrol around the boundaries of their territory and perhaps a bit outside that boundary. When on such patrols, they are tense and eager. They are not looking for food, they are on the warpath. They are looking for an isolated chimp from a neighboring band, and when they find one they attack and kill it. Not for the meat; they generally pound their victim half to death and leave it to crawl away someplace to die. They are trying to exterminate the males in the nearby band and take over its territory and females. In at least one carefully documented case, they did just that.[3] Paradise lost.

There is another ape, the bonobo, which looks like a chimpanzee and is closely related, just a bit smaller. The bonobos don't engage in interband warfare. They are peaceful, and resolve interpersonal and intergroup stress by imaginative uses of heterosexual and homosexual copulation. Paradise regained.

Why the difference? It may have something to do with band size and the regularity of adequate food supplies. The bonobos are inside the big bend of the Congo River, and the geologic evidence suggests that throughout the last five million years, that region has always been tropical rain forest. The chimps are found outside the bend, both to the east and west, and here the geologists say that the Ice Ages have periodically dessicated the rain forest, drying it out to savannah with patches of forest. When food gets sparse, it is no longer possible to travel all the time in bands; survival requires individual foragers to fan out. Individual foragers are more vulnerable than groups. Among the bonobos, Cain doesn't kill Abel because he doesn't have much chance to; outside the Big Bend the situation became quite different for protracted intervals, and so, we infer, was the result.

It would be gratifying if we could trace our human lineage back to the bonobos, rather than to the more warlike chimps, but this isn't so. DNA evidence indicates that the chimpanzee, not the bonobo, is our closest relative.[4] Supporting this view, we are reasonably certain that our hominid ancestors evolved in grasslands with patches of rain forest, not in the rain forest itself.

We've already discussed the fact that while there have been several different kinds of early hominids, they all vanished except for *Homo erectus*. We cannot say for certain why matters worked out this way, for the archeological evidence for the period we are discussing doesn't include indications of how proto-people behaved. All we can say with some assurance is that a certain instinct for killing would have had some survival value. If it had survival value, then the individuals who had more of it were likely to be the ones who survived and passed on their genes to future generations. It is not unreasonable, therefore, to speculate that *H. erectus* was a pretty feisty brute, who had no scruples about killing off the competition.

Enter *Homo sapiens*. There is no reason to believe that the earliest fully evolved humans were less inclined to killing than their forebears. Sapient humans, after all, faced many challenges as they spread out and came to dominate areas already populated by less sapient cousins. Here again, the killer instinct must have provided a powerful boost to human ingenuity and organizational ability in meeting these challenges and overcoming the opposition.

Eventually, human beings arrived at the penultimate stage, where the human killer instinct was unleashed not at more primitive cousins, but against other members of our own species. Perhaps, when our ancestors effectively routed the opposition and established dominance wherever they went, they should have switched gears and set off on a new evolutionary course, like the bonobos. Perhaps they should have resolved way back then to make love, not war, with their fellow humans. But this was not to be.

It is consistent with the central thesis of this book that the killer instinct continued as a powerful human motivator throughout all prehistory and much of the historic era because it continued to have survival value. If we are smart, it is at least partly due to the fact that we are descended from the winners of intergroup conflicts that have been taking place for a hundred thousand years or more. If modern civilization has developed an extraordinarily sophisticated technological base, it is largely because of all the arms races that have occurred between human groups, particularly since the beginning of agriculture.

Let's examine each of these two assertions in more detail.

ARE WE BRIGHT BECAUSE WE USED TO FIGHT?

The injunction "Thou shalt not kill" probably has always been a commonsense rule for almost all societies that have ever existed. Moses didn't invent it, at least not for the first time; it was already an established principle of human conduct. But in earlier times it only applied with full force within the social unit.

Long ago, when human society was organized only at the tribal level, a given tribe could relate to other tribes in various ways; perhaps they traded peacefully or got together for periodic ritual events, or two neighboring groups might even have a pattern of intermarriage. But the chances of a falling-out leading to conflict were usually there and were proportionally greater as the geographic and cultural distance between one tribe and another increased. And once conflict started, the normal taboo against killing was suspended for the duration—as long as the victim was "the enemy."

"Murder" is a term that is applied to killing that lacks official sanction. It is not construed, even now, to apply to killing enemy soldiers in time of war. This distinction holds true, as far as I am aware, at all of the first four levels of altruism I described in the last chapter. There have always been murders, but they have been condemned and punished. There have also always been wars, but the killing that takes place during a war has a different quality. The successful soldier is not a murderer; he may even be a hero.

This dichotomy between two kinds of killing makes sense in the context of my basic point about the evolutionary process undergirding human societies. The culturally defined in-group, whatever its level, cannot tolerate murder within its own ranks.

But it also operates under another equally compelling imperative: once the group or society engages in mortal conflict with another group, it must at all costs win.

I cannot believe there was any extended period in human prehistory that was unmarked by at least a rare outburst of fighting. Ever since our forebears started keeping records, intermittent conflict has been the norm rather than the exception, and there is no reason to assume that this pattern only began when writing was introduced. For the student of evolutionary theory, when one sees a pattern of this consistency, one has to ask, why? What evolutionary purpose does or did that pattern serve? To me, the answer is clear: intermittent conflict between culturally defined groups took over, once our ancestors became fully sapient, as the prime engine of evolution.

The kinds of people who survived conditions of intermittent organized conflict, or war, were the ones most likely to win. Winning during the Paleolithic era was not so much a matter of weapons as it was of teamwork and ability to out-think the enemy. Many of the same skills and qualities that enabled groups of hunters to drive mammoths into bogs and kill them while they were immobilized came into play in intertribal warfare. Courage was important, but so was discipline, a talent for operating as a smoothly functioning member of a team. What is now known as "team spirit" was bred into our ancestors in this formative period.

If Paleolithic humans, like the bonobos, had not had a propensity to get into intertribal fights, if they had always resolved conflicts by making love not war, they might have developed their organizational and tactical skills from hunting alone. Much suffering and needless destruction might have been spared if the killer instinct had been absent. But an argument can be made that if our ancestors had not had that feisty killer instinct in them, their social structures and technologies would have evolved much more slowly. To explain this, we need to introduce the concept of the arms race.

ARMS RACES AND TECHNOLOGICAL INNOVATION

In *The Blind Watchmaker*, Richard Dawkins discusses the impact on biological change through natural selection of what he calls "arms races."[5] One of the simpler versions of such a situation would be the escalation of offensive and defensive capabilities between predator and prey. Both the fastest cheetahs and the fastest antelopes, for example, are the ones that survive and pass on their genes; for each species, the penalties for the slower ones are severe. Dawkins elaborates on various aspects of this principle, including some of the traps its undiscriminating application can lead us into, but concludes: "the arms race idea remains by far the most satisfactory explanation for the existence of the advanced and complex machinery that animals and plants possess."[6]

It seems clear, on a little reflection, that much the same principle holds true for human societies, except that here we are talking about cultural selection. The threat of being overrun and killed or enslaved by a hostile neighboring group can provide as much incentive to get cracking and develop new strengths as any advancing glacier can. And it happens more frequently. Throughout history the arms-race principle as applied between hostile social groups has provided a major incentive for technological and cultural change. It has replaced environmental change as the single most important provoker of human progress.

Remember Pearl Harbor? I do. Nothing galvanized Americans in this century like that aggressive assault and the war into which it launched us. There was a clarity of purpose, a determination, a fierce will to win that all one hundred and fifty million of us shared. It was a good feeling, one that caused us all to do our level best, at least for a few years. We not only won the war, we developed nuclear weapons while other belligerents were developing radar and jet aircraft and much more, while we were all under the influence of this most primal, most atavistic of narcotics.

THE EVOLUTION OF INTERGROUP WARFARE

During the Paleolithic era, tribal conflict emphasized the survival values of character more than weapons technology; discipline, courage, and good teamwork counted for more than better slings and arrows. At least we can infer that from the fact that weapons remained relatively simple up to and into the Neolithic. For millennia before the battle in which he died, people had been making the kind of spear point that killed the warrior whose remains I saw in Jericho.

The introduction of metals changed the technology of war; the first societies that had bronze had a definite edge when their people did battle with groups that didn't have it. The losers can be presumed to have left the battlefield, if they survived at all, with a burning desire to acquire bronze for themselves. The principle of the arms race quickly took over as the dominant principle governing the evolution of war. The arms-race concept applied not only to the weapons themselves but to the ways military units organized to employ them—the Roman phalanx, for example. Military technology surged ahead at an accelerating rate, and is still doing so.

The social implications of war changed along with the

weapons technology. When society split into a dominant warrior/priest/ruler class and a larger group of farmers and villagers, decisions regarding war and peace were monopolized by the elite, although it was often the peasants who paid with their lives. War became a kind of chess game, something between an art and a science. The survivors were the groups led by the most proficient masters of the game of war. Rules of conduct like chivalry evolved to ensure that the elite of the losing side suffered as little as possible.

Nationalism, the fourth level of altruism, changed the nature of war once again. Instead of a passive peasantry manipulated by an elite, the entire nation became engaged. It was as though the commitment of the entire tribe that had existed during the Paleolithic era had reasserted itself, but on a much grander scale. Chivalry died on the battlefields of the First World War. A new and extraordinarily sanguinary epoch began.

The bloodletting that has occurred between states since nationalism first asserted itself has been so great, and the consequences of further warfare so dire, that the most evolved nations have given up the idea that war between them is a viable way of settling conflicts. If this were not the case, then surely, a decade or two after the defeat of Germany and Japan in the mid-1940s, there would have been a Third World War between NATO and the Soviet Union. But by that time it had become fairly clear that the costs of such a war had grown prohibitive, and that there would be no winners. Narrowly, the forces of rationality prevailed. And by the mid-1980s, when the Cold War was winding down, a basic force driving human social and technological evolution began to wind down with it. Local wars persist, but everyone in his or her right mind now agrees that war involving massive exchanges of nuclear weapons must not happen. This is an extremely profound change. If we have to cite only two or three reasons why that butterfly has chosen the twentieth century to begin emerging from its cocoon, the H-bomb, with its resulting impact on thinking about war, has to be included.

MORAL IMPLICATIONS

I cannot work up much enthusiasm over efforts to moralize about what happened in the past. People who lived several generations ago didn't know what we know now, and they shouldn't be considered moral lepers for operating according to the morality of their times rather than ours. So I am comfortable with the notion that the scrappiness our ancestors displayed, despite the suffering it entailed, was on the whole a key factor in getting us out of caves and into jet aircraft. We would not be where we are now if our ancestors hadn't traveled the long and rocky path they did.

This is the spirit in which I have undertaken the disagreeable task of trying to demonstrate that humankind's ancient and atavistic propensity for war conferred an evolutionary advantage. It's entirely different from an attempt to justify war on moral grounds. I am convinced that from now on, everybody should join in condemning war. War is no longer an acceptable way to resolve conflicts.

There are, of course, parts of humankind that have not yet crawled out of the cocoon and are still causing violent problems in various parts of the world. Some of the societies that are still behaving this way may need to be controlled in a forceful manner. But the world community should undertake international police actions reluctantly, and only when humanity as a whole requires that corrective surgery be applied. Medication, not surgery, is normally to be preferred. The purpose is not punishment, but education. The goal is a world order where everyone understands that war is no longer a viable option for any group, anywhere.

NOTES

1. Carleton S. Coon, *Flesh of the Wild Ox* (New York: William Morrow & Co., 1932).

2. Our genus *Homo* probably diverged from the chimp line only about five million years ago, not long in evolutionary terms, and then evolved rapidly. We are distinctly less closely related to gorillas and orangutans, the other main branches of apedom.

3. Richard Wrangham and Dale Peterson, *Demonic Males, Apes and the Origins of Human Violence* (New York: Houghton Mifflin, 1996).

4. The available evidence, which Wrangham and Peterson discuss on pages 40–48 of *Demonic Males*, suggests that physically, modern chimps have changed very little from their (and our) ancestors of five million years ago.

5. Richard Dawkins, *The Blind Watchmaker: Why the Evidence of Evolution Reveals a Universe without Design* (New York: Norton, 1996).

6. Ibid., pp. 170 ff.

CHAPTER 8

RELIGION

In 1971, when I first moved to Kathmandu Valley, there were few paved roads anywhere and very few that extended any distance from the city. One of these very few was a narrow, twisting road that led south-southwest into the neighboring hills, terminating after a few miles at a holy place called Dakshinkali. It was a pretty drive, and there were picnic spots along the way, so we visited it fairly frequently. But we never stayed long at the shrine itself, for the general ambience was a bit too much like an abbatoir to be appetizing.

Dakshinkali was and still is a place where Nepalese villagers and townspeople come to make animal sacrifices. Normally the head of the family takes a rooster to the shrine and decapitates it. These people are making, for them, a real sacrifice, for their

general level of poverty is such that the fowl is a serious investment, not to be given up lightly, even though the owner and his
family get to eat the remains. And the trip, for them, is frequently a long one.

Why are these people doing this? They are doing it because
their people have always done it, because it is an act that propi-
tiates their gods and is expected thereby to enhance their individual hopes and prospects, and because it is a way of doing
something that they believe will give them some influence over
otherwise uncontrollable events. But is this the whole story?

Professor Robert A. Hinde of the University of Cambridge,
England, believes that although religions differ widely, they
share certain structural characteristics.[1] His analysis suggests
that the following elements are integral to any coherent set of
religious beliefs:

Structural Beliefs: "These usually involve an entity or entities
which are related to but are in some sense outside the world in
which we live, have at least some improbable and counter-intu-
itive characteristics, and are usually independent of time."

Why do people subscribe to these beliefs? Probably the most
important reason is that they are taught these beliefs while they
are still in their infancy or early childhood, and have little choice
in the matter. At this early stage, memes are absorbed by a
process popularly known as "imprinting."[2] They register easily,
but are hard to change later on; it is quite unlike information
absorbed later in life, which can be corrected or deleted much
more readily, as a matter of rational choice. It is like language
acquisition: when a child learns to speak, it quickly absorbs the
language of its parents and their peers, but finds it much harder
to learn a new language later on. The phonetic structure of the
native language will persist even after the new vocabulary has
been mastered, accounting for the "foreign" accents we hear.[3]

There are other reasons why many adults continue to adhere to the structural beliefs they learned early in life. However illogical these beliefs may appear when examined rationally, they fill several basic needs, common to all humans. They provide at least the illusion of understanding why things happen, and thereby purport to explain the otherwise inexplicable. In so doing they make it possible to take actions like the sacrifices at Dakshinkali, that give people the sense that they partially control, or at least influence, the forces affecting their destiny. They satisfy a strong emotional need for an enduring relationship with someone who will always be there and on whom they can rely in times of trouble. They can provide the comfort of assurance of life after death. And they can reinforce the individual's comforting sense of belonging to a community while strengthening that community's internal cohesion in its relations with outside groups.

For all these reasons, the true believer accepts the existence of these entities as a matter of faith, not to be questioned. There are, however, other individuals, more inclined to rational analysis and critical thinking, who grow up and discover a certain cognitive dissonance between these beliefs and what they have learned later in life. Some such individuals explicitly and overtly reject the beliefs, but others "go along" with the peer group, keeping their reservations to themselves.

Narratives: Every religion has its stories, fables, gospels, or origin myths, which interweave anecdotal material from everyday life with explanations that extend and exemplify structural beliefs, moral and ethical codes, and rituals. These narratives play an important role in the indoctrination of children, where they operate as a kind of easily assimilated memetic glue that binds the strictly religious memes of the group to the rest of the culture, and vice versa. As the child grows up, it may continue to accept the moral of the narrative while no longer regarding the narrative itself as literally true.

Ritual: This is repetitive behavior, distinct from everyday life, that most people learn as children. It has meaning for those performing it that transcends the actions performed. It can powerfully reinforce other elements of a religion (for example, prayer and Ramadan for Muslims). Many rituals are conducted by religious specialists, whose ability to perform complex ritual acts is one of their identifying characteristics. The priest, the complex ritual, and the structural beliefs reinforce each other. Some rituals serve as rites of passage, punctuating critical events in the lives of individuals.

Ritual need not always be religious; a secular ritual might be the family Thanksgiving dinner in a nonreligious family. Some rituals blend the secular and the religious, as in certain memorial gatherings for those killed in war.

Hinde considers prayer and sacrifice to be specialized forms of ritual behavior. Prayer provides the individual the opportunity to communicate directly with his or her deity. It is a principal channel for meeting the need for a sense of companionship discussed above. Sometimes reinforced by sacrifice, it gives the individual some sense of control over events. Sacrifice, in turn, can serve social ends as well, when it involves a display of wealth or piety that can enhance the individual's standing in the group.

Moral Codes: All the major religious systems include codes of behavior, absorbed early in life as part of the socialization process, which define right versus wrong behavior. Every individual has a mix of impulses and motives ranging from the purely antisocial to the prosocial. By defining what is antisocial and encouraging prosocial behavior, these codes provide essential lubricants for interpersonal relations between members of the culture. They are, as a consequence, critically important to the survivability of the group as a whole, and have evolved within individual cultures as central pillars of the individual's sense of group identity.

There are various elements to any such codes. Some elements are directly related to the religion's structural beliefs and strengthen the individual's determination to resist questioning thoughts ("Thou shalt worship but one God"). A second element reinforces group solidarity ("Thou shalt not kill," which usually refers only to members of the group, not to outsiders with whom the group may be at war). A third category is concerned with the maintenance of social harmony and equilibrium in a more general sense (The Golden Rule). The fact that this latter category can exist without reference to the structural beliefs of the religion in which the child was raised is often lost on that individual, who throughout his life will regard any deviation from his deeply held religious beliefs as "immoral behavior."

Moral codes evolve, along with the cultures they support. In a hierarchical culture they are subject to manipulation from the top, or from a priesthood anxious to shore up its status. There is no such thing as a universal moral code, for they are all products of an evolutionary process, in this case, the evolution of ideas shared by members of a community.

Religious Experience: This is perhaps the most difficult single element of the phenomenon of religion to either categorize or describe. However, there are many documented instances of individuals going through some kind of a moment or period of ecstasy or revelation that strongly reinforces their faith, and frequently has a ripple effect on their peers. These can range from the relatively common experiences of a born-again Christian at a revival meeting to less common mystical and ecstatic experiences, paranormal experiences, and so on.

At this point we need to pause, reflect on our origins, and ask: is the human propensity to engage in religious thought and behavior programmed genetically, or is it exclusively a matter of conditioning, particularly during the individual's early youth? Hinde, Wilson, and others have given this question serious thought and adduced some useful insights. My own view is that a genetically programmed propensity for the kinds of beliefs and practices we have been describing coevolved along with other basic elements of human nature during that long gestation period known as the Paleolithic era. This propensity, or set of "epigenetic rules" to use Wilson's terminology, has survived because it confers survival value, not only on the individual, but on the group. If you share the antipathy of many social scientists for the whole idea of group selection, you are likely to shy away from this concept and try to explain religious behavior entirely in terms of the survival value it confers on the individual. Such explanations have been adduced, and some of them are persuasive, but the whole phenomenon of religious faith and practices makes more sense by far if the concept of group selection is accepted and religion is viewed not just as an individual matter, but also as something that a culturally defined society, taken in its aggregate, finds useful.

It is obvious to me, given my experience in the Middle East and South Asia, that for a culturally defined group operating at the third level of altruism, a coherent and distinctive set of religious beliefs and practices is extremely functional. Many cultures operating at this level use religion as the most important single mechanism for defining their difference from other cultures. The differences between Serbs and Croats, for example, are neither linguistic nor ethnic; they are based primarily on religion and a history of rivalry that grew out of the sectarian differences that developed between them centuries ago. A similar situation obtains, as we have seen, in Lebanon.

The roots of religion may reach far back into our remote ancestral past, but religious forms and practices only reached their finest flower when mainstream human societies graduated from the level of hunter-gatherer tribes to the more elaborate structures of kingdoms and empires. When that happened, religious forms and practices became much more complex. Hierarchies became more elaborate. Doctrinal differences frequently led to unbridgeable splits within formerly cohesive cultural communities. Indeed, seen strictly from the kind of evolutionary perspective proposed in previous chapters of this book, splits over religious doctrine can be said to have played a key role in creating an environment in which culturally defined units fought, bled, and sometimes died in the great competitive game of human social and technological evolution.

But always, no matter what the level of religious complexity might have been, religion served all of the functions Professor Hinde's book described. Its strength did not derive from any particular set of environmental or historical circumstances. Rather, it derived from the fact that on the personal level, religion met basic needs that could not be satisfied in any other way, while on the community level it provided a powerful force for maintaining equilibrium within the group, while strengthening it in its competition with other groups. I think it is fair to say that until recently, the twin pillars of language and religion have been the most efficient, most versatile, and most central features of human culture.

Everything is changing, now that humanity, like that mythical butterfly, is at last coming out of its cocoon. For the first time, the basic premises that have dictated that people shall for the most part be religious are dissolving. We have learned too much by now, about ourselves and our planet, to accept the structural beliefs that undergird most of the old religions. But even more importantly, we no longer need religion as a force to strengthen communities in their competition with other communities, because that competition itself is rapidly becoming dysfunctional.

The old religions are metamorphosing into a new global humanism, a new worldview that is emerging to fill the void. The process has only just begun, and the transition is painful. Most people are reluctant to give up something that has worked so well for so long. The old resentments die hard, as do the most cherished beliefs. So do the entrenched interest groups. But it is happening nonetheless.

Let me close with another anecdote. During my assignment to New Delhi in the late 1950s, I took a couple of days off and drove north to the Himalayan foothills, to Kulu Valley, for the annual festival of the gods. Once each year, the villages in the outer reaches of that valley traditionally took their village gods to Kulu town for a get-together accompanied by feasting and dancing. The gods were idols, elaborate tinsel-bedecked representations of whatever Hindu deity that village chose as its particular protector, and they were carried over the mountain trails and into town on litters, usually four men carrying each. The year I made the visit the assemblage was impressive and colorful. I was glad I had come, but some old-timers there were grumbling. It wasn't like it used to be, they said, the number of gods is off sharply from last year and at this rate the festival will be dead in a few more years. Why? I asked. Land reform, it appeared, was the cause.

Each village god, I was told, had owned a substantial bit of village property, rather like church land in the United States. Part of the rent villagers paid to use this land was the service of lugging the owner into town for the annual jamboree. Land reform took title of the gods' land away and distributed it to the villagers, leaving piety alone to motivate them to carry their god into town when the holiday came around. And such piety, apparently, was in short and dwindling supply.

Is this a good thing? Is there value to this kind of cultural diversity? I shall try to answer these questions, or at least give my opinion, when I discuss cultural diversity in more detail (chapter 13) and when I take a look at religion's future (chapter 21).

NOTES

1. Robert A. Hinde, *Why Gods Persist* (London: Routledge, 1999). I followed Professor Hinde's outline as to the principal components of religion, but except for direct quotes the detailed discussion, while broadly consistent with Hinde's argument, is my own.

2. Strictly speaking, "imprinting" is a term used to describe the process by which young birds learn the characteristics of their species. But the concept is too useful to leave to the exclusive use of ornithologists; like others, I have extended it to humans.

3. For a description of the way a child soaks up the phonetic patterns of its primary language, how that process differs from the one an adult uses to learn a second language, and what adaptive purpose this two-stage process may have served, see Steven Pinker, *The Language Instinct* (New York: W. Morrow and Co., 1995), pp. 293–96.

CHAPTER 9

COMMON SENSE AND THE LAW

For thousands of years philosophers have been searching for the Holy Grails of absolute truth, absolute beauty, absolute justice, and universal moral and ethical standards. You would think they would have found them by now—if they existed at all. Maybe the time has come when we can rephrase the question, from "What are the ideal standards?" to "Why are we looking for them?" or, even better, "Where do our concepts of ethics, beauty, truth, and so forth come from, and what purpose do they serve?"

Every human child is born with certain genetically determined predispositions, or epigenetic rules. Some of these rules are about behavior, as opposed to physical features; they are not precise, but they do help to determine parameters. They incline the individual toward certain ways of behaving without precisely determining the outcome, the way a slope will incline water to flow in one direction rather than the other, while leaving it to the local terrain to determine just where the flow will take place.

One of the more obvious such sets of rules relates to language learning. At a very early age the child soaks up sounds, syntax, and vocabulary from the speech of the older people around him. This language instinct "is a diagnostic and evidently unique human trait . . . and it is the precondition for true culture."[1] At the same time, the child is absorbing nonverbal communication patterns, religious precepts, ethical standards, and other values of his or her community. The totality of what is learned at this stage includes the religious beliefs and other basic elements and assumptions of the group's culture. These basic building blocks are expanded and developed as the individual matures—but the basic pattern is set, and can be unlearned only with great difficulty.

As we have noted, each culture has its own moral code, a set of shared assumptions about correct behavior that regulates conflicts both within the individual and between the individual and the group. Cultural norms keep individuals in step, working together toward goals that are important for the group as a whole, even when they conflict with immediate personal goals. Culture, built on the foundation of language, is learned behavior following genetically prescribed directions. It is central to the package of changes that allowed our ancestors to survive the Paleolithic era and advance to more complex levels of social organization and technology. Without it, we'd be lucky if we were living in caves; we might still be swinging around in trees.

While the child is going through that learning process, its mind is like a blotter; it soaks up certain kinds of impressions indiscriminately, including not only linguistic patterns, but what is good and bad and what is right and wrong. It learns by observing the behavior of the people around it, by being chastised when it violates their code, and from their mythology. The child stores much of this knowledge at a subconscious level, so that later in life he or she is only dimly aware of it, if at all. If the process is incomplete or unsuccessful and later in life that person turns into a horse thief or shoplifter, people will shake their heads and say he "just wasn't brought up right," or that she was "culturally deprived."

As it matures, the child expands and diversifies this subconscious set of values and behavioral standards by absorbing elements of those experiences that fit best into the evolving framework of his or her persona. What started as a fairly simple listing of dos and don'ts becomes more elaborate, and comes to include issues of "what works" as well as "what is right." He or she ends up with something peers recognize as wisdom or good judgment. That person can be said to have integrated successfully with the culture of the group.

It is useful to think of common sense as culture, seen from the inside out. It is what the group perceives as its commonly shared distilled wisdom, the ideas and precepts that everybody knows, or ought to. It blends the ethical and the pragmatic. It draws on subconscious levels of training and experience to inform conscious decisions regarding current issues or problems. To the extent that an individual's actions conform with this body of common sense, he or she is perceived by other members of the group as acting "sensibly." When the contrary is true, "Well, that fellow just ain't got no sense at all!"

Common sense within a society changes as that society evolves. It used to be common sense in much of the world that slavery was a right and natural aspect of human organization. Even cannibalism was once accepted as right and sensible in a few of the world's societies. In this century a commonsense perception has emerged that the environment is endangered and must be protected. Can we predict that global overpopulation will eventually lead to a global commonsense perception that procreation is too important a matter to be left entirely to the judgment of individual parents?

Now we are able to answer the questions posed at the beginning of this chapter. Values, ethical standards, moral precepts, like language, are what a given society says they are. There is no absolute truth out there in the firmament waiting to be discovered. We humans are on our own. And looked at in the hindsight of history, we haven't been doing too badly. Our standards have evolved enormously, and are still changing, as we grope our way into an unforeseeable future. Because we are a social species, we are perforce ethical and caring. And we shall continue to be in the future, because that is our genetic inheritance. In fact, we can expect that our descendants will become more caring and ethical in the future, as we come to understand the causes of past strife and discord, and as we come to agree on the urgent need to cooperate to avoid planetary destruction.

COMMON SENSE AND THE LAW

Common sense, as we have noted, is what keeps culturally defined groups together. It validates behavior that enhances the survivability of the group, by ensuring cooperation where cooperation is essential for survival. But it is a framework within which conduct is judged for its rightness, not a complete catalogue of what to do in all circumstances. It is a syntax for behavior, not a complete vocabulary. Issues constantly arise that fall within areas of ambiguity. Was that hungry child stealing when he pinched an apple from his neighbor? Yes. Should he be put in the same category as the adult who stole his neighbor's horse? Obviously not, that's only common sense.

Small hunter-gatherer tribes had relatively little trouble applying common sense as they perceived it to concrete problems. There was a "fit" between culture and the environment. Jean-Jacques Rousseau's noble savage didn't need lawyers. Perhaps that explains a certain contemporary nostalgia for a mythic early age where life was simple and uncomplicated, a nostalgia that should, however, be tempered by realization that life in those days also tended to be "nasty, brutish, and short."

As culturally defined groups enlarged, and particularly when the dawn of the Neolithic era caused populations to explode in size and density, the old "fit" between common sense and the environment began to come apart at the seams. Something more specific was needed by way of culturally imposed dos and don'ts, if culture was to continue in its role as mediator between the individual and the group. The human capacity to modify its behavior patterns in order to meet new challenges was put to the test, and rose to the challenge. Culture spawned a new offspring, "the law," and the first lawyers appeared on the scene, disguised for the most part as shamans or medicine men.

The law is a codification of rules of conduct and rights that is formally recognized by society or prescribed by the authority in a state. It distinguishes between what is permitted and what is prohibited. Where common sense is general, the law is specific. It is as complex as the society it regulates, and provides guidance that is as precise as its human framers can make it. It is, therefore, frequently comprehensible only to specialists. It is devoid of humor and other graces. Common sense, by contrast, is simple and easy to understand. It is often expressed in generalities and homilies, both of which apply to a given situation in parable form, more poetic than precise. It is good-humored and often witty.

Like common sense, laws evolve when changes are introduced into the ways people live. If you are in charge of a city state in Mesopotamia in the Bronze Age, and have just developed your people's first major irrigation system, you are going to need laws and regulations governing who gets how much of the newly available water. Traditional common sense won't resolve your problems by itself. Similarly, a more modern ruling authority may find itself facing, for the first time, the problem of too many radio stations for the available frequencies. Again, the answer is likely to be new laws or regulations. Now we are facing, for the first time, a need for new laws to regulate genetic engineering.

Individual laws can be more or less respected. In the United States, most people exceed the speed limit on superhighways while respecting the requirement to stop for a red light. (Why? It's just a matter of common sense.) But as a commonsense proposition, in any reasonably well-organized society, there is a very broadly shared respect for the law, the law of the land taken as a whole. Any individual who displays a generic contempt for the law is regarded with suspicion by his neighbors, and if he translates his contempt by actions that consistently break the law, his peers gang up on him and put him away, using whatever mechanism the law provides. For no society can tolerate too many out-and-out outlaws in its midst and survive.

A BRIEF HISTORICAL ANALYSIS

This dichotomy between common sense and the law provides an interesting lens through which to look at human prehistory and history.

During the many millennia of humanity's infancy, when there were only a few tens of thousands of hunters and gatherers scattered in small tribes, life may have been harsh but there were compensations. There were, as far as we know, no lawyers. Shamans managed the rites of passage that marked critical phases in the lives of individuals and presided over whatever passed for religious observances. Religion and ethics were everybody's property; they merged with common verbal and nonverbal behavior patterns in everyone's mind, forging a powerful sense of group solidarity. Personal behavior was regulated as much if not more than it is for modern people, but the regulations were for the most part understood, and accepted by all as common sense.

By the time of city-states and empires, shamans were replaced by priests who developed elaborate hierarchies. These priesthoods, like modern bureaucracies, tended over time to develop increasingly complicated ways of answering essentially simple questions. As a particular priesthood matured, therefore, its doctrine became obscure on the one hand, and distinctive on the other. Godhead was divided not into two or four, but precisely three parts. Theft of a horse was punishable in a precisely determined way. Women had to dress so their ankles didn't show, or wear veils, or whatever. This pursuit of complexity served several purposes, including that of adding to the ways by which culturally identified groups distinguished themselves from each other.

And why not? The tendency of priests and lawmakers to make laws more complex, and therefore more group-specific, arose at the beginning of a long period during which the process of evolution was powered to a large extent by conflict between different cultures. The individual was loyal to his tribe, kingdom, or nation, and ready to fight the group next door (which may have differed in language, perhaps, or ethnicity, or religion), because he was brought up that way. It was common sense for that time. But common sense wasn't specific enough to do the job by itself. A lot of it might be shared by the people next door, in the rival kingdom. Each individual's common sense therefore had to be reinforced by a more specific, shaped body of beliefs, a complex of dos and don'ts unique to his own group, which priests and other specialists drummed into him throughout his life.

Throughout this long period of intercultural conflict, there was normally a symbiotic relationship between the priests/lawmakers and the temporal rulers. The priests defined and legitimized the authority of the rulers, who in turn applied this authority in ways that assured that the priesthood would flourish. This buddy system took many forms, and sometimes it broke down, but it was effective, stable, and normal. Perhaps its greatest strength was that it held ordinary people in thrall, by preventing most of them from even thinking about revolt in the first place, and justifying the use of extreme force against the few who did.

What this meant in practice was that the common sense of the majority of the population didn't play any significant role in either formulating or executing the law of the land. There was a second common sense, that of the priests and rulers, and that was the only one that mattered. With few exceptions, most of the members of our species throughout most of humanity's long history, from the Neolithic era until at least the eighteenth century, were subjugated to a privileged few who shaped the law for their own benefit and brooked no opposition from the majority. The law was supreme, legitimized by doctrines like the divine right of kings and papal infallibility. If you happened to believe that the will of the majority was important too, you either shut up or were in trouble.

The philosophical opposite to this oligarchic alliance of kings, priests, and lawmakers is humanism, which in its essence is a regard for every individual's needs and opinions that cuts across class and cultural lines. It was inconceivable that ruling oligarchies could suppress humanist thinking at all times and everywhere; indeed, the earliest stirrings of humanist thought appear in philosophical writings going back to ancient times.[2]

By the eighteenth century, there were enough educated people outside the ruling classes, with enough knowledge about the world, to develop a distinct political ferment. All sorts of solutions were proposed to the perceived problem of the many being oppressed and exploited by the few. The most inclusive of these centered on some form of humanist ethic; Rousseau's *Social Contract* and Locke's *Two Treatises on Government* come to mind. This kind of thinking was basic to the seminal documents that accompanied the birth of the United States of America, notably the Declaration of Independence.

The concepts of liberty, respect for the individual, democracy, separation of church and state—all these and more, stand in explicit opposition to tyranny. They all represent humanist rejection of the old system of exploitation by an alliance of temporal and spiritual leaders. And while they also represent respect for the law, they stand for the basic and revolutionary idea that the law is just and right only when it is validated, not by a priesthood, but by the common sense of the entire society.

COMMON SENSE AND WORLD OPINION

As we have seen, there is nothing immutable or eternal about common sense, ethics, and morality. They are all culture-specific. They all vary according to time and place. We look back, say, to the Aztec civilization in pre-Columbian times, and marvel at how different they were from us.

If we cast our net more broadly, we see, in the X-ray light of hindsight, that common sense tends to become more congenial to our own values when the constituency that shares it broadens. The larger and more inclusive the group, the more "sensible." The more you think like the fellows on the other side of the river, the harder it is to hate them. The world would indeed be a better place if everyone shared the common sense of enlightened, modern humanists. Warfare would end, because it wouldn't "make sense" to the adversaries. So would environmental degradation, abuse of human rights, and a whole host of other problems harking back to the bad old days when nations went to war, and individuals thought only of the "bottom line."

This may sound utopian, but it is happening. It is one aspect of the fact that humanity is finally beginning to crawl out of the cocoon that has embraced it for so many millennia. It is one of the subtler and more important reasons for optimism about the long-term prospects of our species.

NOTES

1. Edward O. Wilson, *Consilience* (New York: Vintage Books, 1999), p. 145.
2. Corliss Lamont, *The Philosophy of Humanism*, 7th ed. (New York: Continuum, 1990), pp. 30ff.

CHAPTER 10

A WOMAN'S PLACE

It may well be that my courage exceeds my judgment, but I would like now to continue this retrospective with a sketchy description of the role women have played in the past evolution of human society.

PREHISTORY

Let us start at the beginning, when our species first began to evolve out of apehood. According to some theories, the main impetus for the development of the larger and more efficient brain that made us human was the requirement that men pursue and kill large mammals in the savannah. Some feminist thinkers, however, have argued that it was women, not men, who led the evolutionary march that made our ancestors human. Erect posture, according to them, evolved from the woman's need to have both hands free while gathering food, and to carry it home so it could be both shared and stored.

I refuse to take sides. Probably as the scientific community accumulates more evidence, this gender-based debate will lose its force, and we will come to the view that both approaches to this issue are partly true—and that other factors as well entered into our evolution from ape to hominid. I would be surprised if it didn't result from adaptive change by both sexes.

Another issue concerns the selection process. When it comes to deciding who mates with whom, who does the deciding, the male or the female? This is even trickier than the first issue, but it does have a bearing on the evolutionary process, if we can judge by what we have learned from studying other species. Take, for example, the chimpanzee: it appears that the males of a troop are ranked in an informal hierarchy, with the number-one male pretty much deciding which female or females he wants for his partner. If you doubt that, just ask him. But who influences his decision? Much goes on behind the scenes. Observers have established that the female chimp, through networking, body language, grooming, and other more or less subtle techniques, plays a substantial role in determining who mates with whom. She prefers to mate with a male that is distinguished by physical size and prowess on the one hand, and status within the band on the other. So the female does have a say in these matters, one way or another, and therefore there is an element of sexual selection among male chimpanzees that is based not just on male dominance but partly on female choices.[1]

The early female hominid paid a price for assuming an erect posture, in that the birth canal became somewhat constricted.

With the evolution of *H. erectus* and finally *H. sapiens*, the problem of childbearing was aggravated by the increase in the size of the baby's head. These changes required that birth occur earlier in the total life cycle of the individual than is common for most other species. This didn't mean an absolute shortening of the duration of the gestation period, but rather a reduction in the ratio between the gestation period and the total time the child was dependent on parental support. It meant that after birth, the infant required parental attention for years longer than a baby chimp. Therefore, early humans formed pair bonds, because the infant was more likely to survive his protracted childhood if the father was still present to help the mother provide food and protection. This added a specifically human criterion for our female ancestors to use in selecting a mate, the factor called "male paternal investment," or MPI. Human females, more than their chimpanzee cousins, looked for whatever evidence they could find of fidelity and commitment when they selected a mate. This "partnership," however, was often felt more strongly by the females than by the males, who remained somewhat polygamous despite their commitment to a specific female.[2]

Another question bearing on the woman's role in the Paleolithic era concerns the food supply. How much of our ancestral nourishment in those days came from vegetable matter, roots and fruits and such like, and how much came from the meat of animals we hunted? Gathering vegetable products, according to most authorities, was mostly women's work, while hunting appears always to have been primarily a male prerogative. Some authorities postulate that in early times food gathering was central to our ancestors' survival, while hunting was at best marginal. This is arguable, at least as a general proposition. Many early human bands may have depended more on the food the women gathered than they did on what the men killed; this probably varied from place to place and time to time. But even when hunting was episodic and most of the regular diet was vegetarian, hunting must have been important, not only for protein but for the supply of skins and bones and other useful materials. We can infer from the archeological evidence, including a vast array of animal bones that have been roasted and cracked open, that our forebears were in fact hunters as well as gatherers. The evidence to be inferred from surviving hunter/gatherer groups is less conclusive. The Bushmen in the Kalahari Desert are largely foragers, not hunters, but in the highly marginal land they have been pushed into there isn't much to hunt anyway. Almost certainly both sides in this argument are partly right.

We have archeological evidence that religion in the late Paleolithic era and early Neolithic era was sometimes based on worship of female deities, the "earth mother" or mother-goddess theme. One school of thought takes this as evidence that throughout this period societies were matriarchal; there was no male domination. Women, not men, invented agriculture and were the first to domesticate animals. Neolithic societies that flourished in the Middle East and central Europe were peaceful and far more advanced than our contemporary male-dominated histories recognize. Arts flourished, and societies advanced. These were graceful, nurturing times, according to this view, but they were destroyed when male-dominated tribes swept out of the steppes and started the bloodshed and mayhem that still plagues our once-idyllic, female-oriented planet.[3]

I find it difficult to believe that the Neolithic era was the peaceful golden age the paradigm in the preceding paragraph suggests. The flint spear point at Jericho, which I saw sticking out from the ribs of a ten-thousand-year-old male, suggests otherwise, as does everything else I have learned about the subject. And the assertion that during our prehistory women invented

everything worthwhile, including agriculture and animal husbandry, seems open to question. But things were quite different
then, from what they were to become, and the balance between
the genders may well have been more even.

THE HISTORIC PATTERN: MALE DOMINATION

Throughout *recorded* history, our species has been largely male-
dominated. Some societies for which we have records have been
matriarchal, but the vast majority have been patriarchal. Poly-
theistic religions had both gods and goddesses, but usually the
most important god in the pantheon was a male. The deity as
defined in its own way by each of the three major monotheistic
religions (Judaism, Christianity, and Islam) is unabashedly
male. The Koran and associated Islamic texts define the
woman's value with some precision: it is half that of the male in
such matters as inheritance, testimony in court cases, and com-
pensation to the family in case of death. The woman's role was
increasingly marginalized, and in extreme cases she was little
better than a slave. The major actors on the world's stage, the
kings and warriors and priests, were almost all men. And so it
has remained until modern times.

The transition from hunter-gatherer bands through Neolithic farming communities to Bronze Age cities and Iron Age
empires profoundly altered the ways our ancestors organized
themselves into social, political, and economic groups. It would
be surprising if such profound transformations had not also
affected male-female relationships. But why did most of the
newer, more complex societies that emerged out of the transition from humanity's infancy to its childhood follow this pat-

tern of increasing male domination? What was there about the
changes in the ways people lived that necessitated this direction
of change? We know that modern women are just as intelligent
as their male counterparts (some modern women would say
more so); we know that their organizational skills are at least on
a par with those of men; and they are not less articulate. They
are at least as important when it comes to propagation of the
race—more so, in that the individual male is more expendable.
All this was as true in the post-Neolithic period as it is today.

   There are several theories that address this question. My
own is based on the fact that there was a great deal of warfare
during this transitional period. New means of production led to
increased population pressures while new technologies and
forms of social organization led to less stable intertribal relations. It became possible for a given group to acquire or develop
new weapons and a new approach to military organization, and
to conquer vast areas containing many times its own population. Empire building on this scale was inconceivable in Paleolithic times and as far as we know it didn't occur on any major
scale during the Neolithic era. And the kind of combat it
entailed was clearly man's work, not woman's. The edge the
male had in physical strength was decisive in those days of
hand-to-hand combat, and the fact that he was relatively dis-
pensable added to the logic of his assuming the fighter's role,
almost to the complete exclusion of women. If half the male
population went off to the wars and only a fraction came back,
never mind, the surviving males had more than one woman
each to breed with, and the group *as a whole* survived essentially
as well, demographically speaking, as it would have if everybody had stayed home.

   When one group physically conquered another group the
victors usually spared the losing side's women. This both

reflected and reinforced a growing tendency to look on women as a valuable kind of property rather than as partners. When the annihilation of the losing side's men was fairly complete, the losing side's women often ended up as concubines or second-class wives of the victorious warriors. They then contributed to the cultural broadening of the victors by inculcating the tribe's children with some of the more useful values and techniques of the losers.

It was not a way of life we now regard with approval, but it worked well for its time. It created an environment in which cultural selection operated at an accelerated rate to favor the development of technological skills as well as group loyalty, resourcefulness, and courage. But it didn't do much for the women of that period, other than to encourage stoicism, and perhaps a sharpened sense of how to work their will with their menfolk through subtlety and indirection. No, this period was a long night for the female of our species.

FIRST SIGNS OF A MORE EQUAL PARTNERSHIP

I see a direct relationship between the first important stirrings of the humanist impulse, with its questioning of the divine rights of kings and priests, and the development of more equal relations between the sexes. The old religions, as we have noted, were for the most part male-oriented. If you want a sociological history of female bashing, both the Old and the New Testaments of the Bible can provide it richly. It is no coincidence that in my country the most fervent female opponents of modern feminist movements, including freedom of choice, the Equal Rights Amendment, and combining careers with family, are women of the far-right Evangelical Christian movement. They are the quislings of their gender, in this era.

We'll look at the *current* status of women in more detail later. Suffice it here to note that the so-called gender revolution relates to more than just the increasing acceptance of humanism as opposed to theism. It ties in with just about all the other radical changes that are taking place at present, in human society and in the way our species relates to the environment. Equal rights for women is a new thread, a new color, a new pattern that is being woven into the grand design. It is a new melody, or perhaps the resurrection of a very ancient one, that we can now hear emerging in the great symphony of humankind. It fits together and harmonizes with other new variations on old themes; and together they are producing a climactic new synthesis. The tree of human life is in the process of producing some amazing new fruit.

NOTES

1. Robert Wright, *The Moral Animal: Why We Are the Way We Are* (New York: Random House, Vintage, 1994), esp. chap. 3.

2. Ibid., p. 90: Sexual dimorphism, i.e., difference in size between male and female, is a good index of the intensity of sexual selection among males, which in turn is a sign of how polygamous the species is. This is because in a highly polygamous species, the big powerful male usually gets to father the most offspring, while this factor does not apply nearly as much in a more monogamous species. We are much less dimorphic than gorillas, and less so than chimps, but more so than the highly monogamous gibbons.

3. Riane Eisler, *The Chalice and the Blade* (San Francisco: Harper & Row, 1987).

B. S. Guha (*right*), director of the Tribal Research Institute at Ranchi, Bihar, India, with the author's father.
All photos are by the author.

Nepali porters are tough. This one is carrying heavy planks up a mountain trail.

Asur dancers in India celebrate the visit of the author.

Striking a population balance: a Newar within Kathmandu Valley, Nepal.

A porter crossing a river in the Nepalese hills. He carries a heavy load across a raging torrent on a flimsy bridge. Like humanity as a whole, these days...

When a Newar in the Kathmandu Valley reaches the age of seventy-seven years, seven months, and seven days (they usually don't), she is feted like a young bride, carried around town in a parade, and relieved of household chores from then on.

His Holiness Kyentse Rinpoche, a highly revered and beloved Tibetan Buddhist ecclesiastic and friend of the author, who, prior to his recent death, lived outside Kathmandu. He was the Dalai Lama's teacher.

The annual festival in Kulu Valley, northern India, when villagers from all around bring their gods to town to celebrate.

"Best Guide," the Shahsevan villager who taught the author mountaineering in northwestern Iran.

Kurds in Mahabad in northwestern Iran.

Cultural contrast—donkey and burden in Fez, Morocco.

The "fantasia," a custom in Morocco where Berbers race their prize horses while firing their guns in the air. In recent years, the race has become commercialized for Western tourists.

Looking north toward the high Himalayan range, from the top of Shivpuri on the northern rim of Kathmandu Valley. A view for the millenium.

CHAPTER 11

INFORMATION'S TWO REVOLUTIONS

Human progress can be defined largely in terms of the changes in the concepts or frames through which groups of people view themselves and the world around them. Discomfort stimulates questioning, assumptions are discarded, solutions are worked out, and new assumptions modify old frames.

An early stimulus for this was climatic change: as the glaciers advanced and the climate got colder, people had to adapt or perish. More recently, the principal stimuli for revisions of commonly held frames have been generated *within* humanity rather than imposed from outside. Conflict between groups and technological innovation have been the most important agents of change. Now the wheel is turning full circle: thanks to our reckless plundering of the planet we inhabit, physical changes in the environment are approaching that are as threatening to modern societies as the glaciers were to our ancestors.

But understanding *why* frames change is not the same as understanding *how* they change. I believe that the principal mechanism through which such basic changes are effected is creative thinking. Someone looks at an array of data and sees in it a pattern that has not previously been identified. The pattern is tested and found valid. It is then incorporated into the totality of human knowledge and experience, which becomes that much richer.

If one accepts this definition of creative thinking, and its role in the evolutionary process, the next step is to identify the factors or conditions that facilitate such thinking. It is immediately apparent that the key factors all involve information. The first factor is the total volume of information a given society possesses at a given time—the more there is, the larger the number of possible patterns. The second factor is access: if the individual thinker can't get at the information that is available somewhere else, he or she may not be able to see its patterns. The third factor is the ability of the creative individual not only to gain access to a wide variety of information but to organize it, to marshal it in rows and series, as it were, and then shuffle the deck and do it again in different ways, all the time scanning for patterns. The fourth factor is the ability to store and preserve the results of one's creative thinking so that they become accessible to others, including other creative thinkers.

Conditions for our remote ancestors were extremely hostile to creative thinking, on all but the most elementary levels. Each individual had access only to the information his own five senses provided, plus the events and interpretations that a small circle of tribal partners conveyed to him. People did the best they could under the circumstances. Specialists—shamans and storytellers—sometimes displayed enormous powers of recall, telling tales of the past that constituted a kind of tribal oral history. But memory alone is a limited way of storing information, even in the hands of specialists.

Biologically speaking, these early humans were as intelligent as we are. And within their limitations they did remarkable things with toolmaking, hunting and gathering techniques, and adapting to changing environments. But their inventiveness was limited by the paucity of information available.

Groups in particularly well-endowed environments developed agriculture, and populations got denser. The need for more complex organizations created a parallel need for better ways than the old oral traditions to store and access information. Along came writing, first in fairly unsatisfactory forms, finally in the alphabetic version. Writing was the first quantum breakthrough in humanity's ability to manage information. It was a major contributor to the upheaval that ended the Paleolithic era and launched our species on a new trajectory.

Writing transformed society. It changed the environment for creative thinking by exponentially expanding opportunities for recording, collecting, observing, storing, and classifying or rearranging information.

The people of literate societies were so different from those of preliterate societies that in a cultural sense they became a different species. Even today, with all our hindsight, it is impossible for us to think like preliterate humans. My anthropologist father tried, and from a descriptive point of view he did pretty well. He could mingle with them and observe how they behaved; and he could correlate different parts of what he observed. But he was still outside looking in, rather than inside. Humanity had crossed a great gulf, and neither he nor anyone else on the forward side of that gulf has ever been able to think the same way the people left behind do or did.

A further exponential explosion in the volume of information available for creative thinking, and in the capacity to store, access, and organize it, came with the invention of the printing press. Historians have picked away at the causal relationship between that development and the subsequent acceleration in the rate of technological and social change in what has come to be known as the modern world.

Now we find ourselves crossing another major divide, and entering brand-new territory. I refer, of course, to the current computer-driven information revolution. This is a major revolution, on a par with the invention of writing. Its potentials are not yet fully revealed, but are likely to be particularly profound for storage, access, and management of information. Creative thinking, along with many other forms of thinking, planning, and organizing, will benefit enormously.

The computer revolution has capped a wave of other recent changes, mostly technological in origin, like the telegraph, the telephone, radio, and television. These changes have created unprecedented wealth for the world's more favored nations; abolished space and time for communication; vastly reduced the friction of space and time for travel and transportation; substantially extended the individual's probable life span; made wars between the major powers unthinkable; and given man for the first time the capability of committing planetary suicide simply by continuing to do what comes naturally.

It's time for a break, another anecdote:

I first visited Nepal in July 1958, a scant decade after it had chosen to stop being a hermetically sealed medieval kingdom and open its gates to foreigners. I found an old Nepali journalist nursing a whiskey at a bar, and waxing nostalgic. He told me the following tale:

Back in the mid-1930s, when I was the Reuters correspondent, there was an important jailbreak. I knew of it because one of the political prisoners who escaped came and hid in my house. I wanted to report it to London but knew I'd have to get the prime minister's permission first. So I called on the PM and he said yes, go ahead and report it. I wrote out the report and sent it by Morse code over the single copper wire that connected Kathmandu to the Indian border. There a clerk on our side of the border typed it up and sent it by runner across to India. Another clerk on the Indian side then tapped the message out in Morse code again, and it went to Delhi. Eventually it reached London and was picked up by the press. The Foreign Office cabled the British resident in Kathmandu who then queried the prime minister. The prime minister then remarked to me, "Isn't it amazing, this word went all the way to London and back and it only took a week!"

We've come a long way, and in a very short time.

All these extraordinary developments, most of them occurring within living memory, are interconnected. War, politics, economics, gender relations, religion, moral standards, philosophy, art, and virtually all other aspects of the human condition are all going through a single unified metamorphosis. They are all in it together. Humanity is merging into one vast multicultural ocean, while the rivers that fed into it and created it are drying up.

As parts of this new ocean, we can look back on the rivers that created us with nostalgia, but without regret.

PART II
FOREGROUND

CHAPTER 12

CULTURE WARS
AND THE GLOBAL VILLAGE

Cultural hostility, as opposed to culture itself, remains a major problem in many parts of the world. It may be that this kind of conflict will slowly die out with the passage of time, since cultural conflicts depend for their sustenance on dehumanizing the out-group, and the advent of the information era is making ignorance about the other side harder to maintain and easier to dispel. But we aren't there yet. There's a rocky road ahead to a general condition of intercultural harmony.

One of the higher callings for young people in the coming century will be working to increase intercultural understanding. Such people will be the missionaries of the age, spreading light among groups still mired at the third level of altruism by giving them a modern vision of the new global community. It will be an uphill job, but time will be on their side, along with the whole general thrust of human social evolution.

I have already provided several examples of intercultural strife from my own experience. Now, as we begin to survey the contemporary scene, we can take a somewhat more inclusive look at the world and review the ways culture-based differences are still playing themselves out in some of the world's present trouble spots.

COMMUNALISM IN SYRIA AND LEBANON

Do you remember the story in chapter 1 about Michel Husseini, my Arabic teacher in Damascus, and his reaction when one of his students blew his brains out? Michel was a member of the Maronite community. The Maronite Church is an independent branch of the Catholic Church and embraces most of the many Lebanese who are Christian. During the French mandate, between the First and Second World Wars, the French supported the Maronites, who effectively dominated Lebanon's political life. After the Second World War the French mandate ended and the numerically superior Lebanese Muslims increasingly asserted themselves. But the process of redistributing political power was painful, especially for the Maronites, and much bitterness resulted. Michel's response was all the lesson I needed to impress on me the intensity of religious feelings in Syria and Lebanon.

Thanks to Michel, I was able to understand the Shatila massacre. In September 1982, Israel invaded Lebanon and took over Beirut. They had split Lebanon not only territorially, but to a large extent along religious lines, for they had worked out an alliance with the Phalange, an armed force of Maronite

Lebanese. Shatila was a sprawling camp of Palestinian refugees just outside Beirut. The Israelis told the Phalangist forces to go in and clean the place up, and they did. The resident population was slaughtered, brutally—about 800 to 1,000 people by some counts, mostly women and children.[1]

Does anyone doubt that the Middle East is still a cauldron of hatred? Does anyone share the view of that well-meaning U.S. senator who once visited the area and asked plaintively: "Why don't these Israelis and Arabs just sit down and work this out in a good Christian spirit?"

ETHNIC MINORITIES IN THE FORMER SOVIET UNION

The USSR inherited czarist Russia's imperial rule over a large variety of distinct cultural groups, and for nearly a century the iron fist of the communist state forced these peoples to coexist in what superficially at least seemed to be harmony. Once the Soviet grip loosened, however, the underlying reality asserted itself, and many of the larger culturally defined groups hived off as independent nations. Instantly, each developed a distinct personality, based on the very factors I have identified as constituents of distinctive cultures: linguistic, ethnic, territorial, historic, and so forth. The Kyrghiz and the Kazakhs are similar in many ways, for example, but the first group lives in the mountains and the other in the plains, and over the centuries each has evolved its own way of life. Now each of these nations has its own embassy in Washington, doling out visas to American businessmen and tourists. Meanwhile, distinct cultural groups in the Caucasus remained under Moscow's control, for various complicated reasons, and some of them didn't like that at all. Mother

Russia still has trouble with what is left of its brood, especially, these days, in the fractious Muslim province of Chechnya.

In Chechnya, a hardy collection of Muslim mountain people have been defying the enormously greater power of a modern state, Russia, apparently in contradiction of the general rule that when two cultures collide, the larger and more sophisticated one prevails. Their initial success in holding off the Russian armed forces will probably not last forever, but the fact that they succeeded even initially is remarkable, and attributable at least partly to the demoralization of Russian society and its armed forces in the current post-Soviet turmoil.

THE KURDISH PROBLEM

Like the Chechnyans, the Kurds are a hardy lot of mountaineers who have had a lot of experience fighting, for when there is no external threat to rally against, their tribes frequently feud with each other. There is a story that back in the 1920s one of the larger Kurdish tribes lured the main force of the Iraqi army into a box canyon and cut it off. Baghdad, facing the loss of the whole unit, produced a bag or two of gold and with it bribed another Kurdish tribe to attack in the rear, thus liberating the Iraqi force. Such internal divisions have been the Kurds' Achilles' heel for a very long time, and continue to this day to hamstring their efforts to achieve unity and independence.

The other problem the Kurds face, which differentiates them from the Chechnyans, is that they oppose not one major power but three: Turkey, Iraq, and Iran, all of which have substantial Kurdish minorities. So these modern states not only play individual Kurdish factions off against each other within their own boundaries; they also play games against each other, using various Kurdish factions as pawns. I sympathize with the Kurds; when I was consul in Tabriz, Iran, in the mid-sixties I met and dealt with them a good deal, rather more than I was supposed to. But if I were one of them, I would see little hope for the future, given their geopolitical circumstances and their apparently incurable inability to work together.

THE BALKANS: "ETHNIC CLEANSING" IN KOSOVO

The former Yugoslavia, like the former Soviet Union, was comprised of culturally distinct groups which for the most part had ancestral reasons to hate each other but were forced to cooperate by Tito's iron hand. During its heyday, the Yugoslav Foreign Ministry apportioned all its diplomatic slots, not just the ambassadorial ones but other personnel down the line, by community, very much the way the positions were allocated between Greeks and Turks for the embassies of Cyprus in New York and Washington. When the federation broke up, all hell broke loose—or something closely approximating it. In Bosnia, the world watched while militant Serbs took over Srbrenica and marched off hundreds of Bosnian Muslim males to their deaths. This atavistic procedure of slaughtering the enemy's able-bodied men shocked the world. When the process was repeated in Kosovo, on an even larger scale, the world responded. This was not an ordinary civil war, it was genocide, also known as "ethnic cleansing."

From any reasonably modern point of view, the worst outcome of a collision between two cultures is when the stronger one consciously tries to achieve a "final solution" by killing or driving out everyone on the other side. The aggressors are obsessed with the "us vs. them" syndrome and don't regard the victims as human. What they are doing is, for them, the highest expression of patriotic zeal or service to their god, or perhaps the fulfillment of some kind of millennial myth. But for anyone else, any third party, what they are doing is murder on a mass scale. It is the ultimate crime against humanity. Nowadays we call it genocide, or "ethnic cleansing," and distinguish it from other forms of civil war and insurrection.

One might think that humanity as a whole had graduated beyond this stage. Indeed, for a while the prevailing opinion in the United States and Western Europe was that the Holocaust was so horrible, so roundly and universally condemned, that nothing like it could ever happen again. Well, yes, there was ethnic cleansing in Cambodia, but it was far away and only spottily covered by the media. Then there was the slaughter in Rwanda, but again, this seemed pretty remote. But when the former Yugoslavia erupted, it was no longer possible for us just to hold our noses and look the other way. This was genocide, and it was happening to people who looked just like most of us, and in our own backyard.

The NATO response to Serbian ethnic cleansing in Kosovo was appropriate. Someone had to stand up and say enough, this kind of resolution of ancestral quarrels must henceforth be banned, eliminated from the human repertoire. Yes, it would have been better if the United Nations had taken over; and yes, somebody should have stepped in to stop the genocide in Central Africa, or even Cambodia. But none of those outcomes was possible, for various reasons. That was no excuse for not acting when the Serbs began their ethnic cleansing in Kosovo. When NATO stepped in and drew a line in the sand, it was a watershed, and now humanity as a whole is a little better off. There may be more instances elsewhere of ethnic cleansing, but at least we now have a precedent for stopping it and punishing the perpetrators.

KASHMIR AND CYPRUS, AND OTHER SUCH CONFLICTS

The Kosovo crisis was a clash between two groups of people— Serbs and Albanians—fated to live in the same space but separated by religion, language, ethnicity, and a long history of mutual hostility. It was a brutal reminder of the kinds of cultural collisions that have punctuated the long and violent history of human social evolution since prehistoric times. It was an atavistic event that reminded us of our violent roots in a manner so vivid that it penetrated all our considerable powers of self-deception and rationalization, and forced us to react.

The conflicts over Kashmir and Cyprus are a bit more complicated. The countries engaged in these continuing confrontations—India and Pakistan over Kashmir, and Greece and Turkey over Cyprus—are organized not at the third level of altruism but at the fourth. There has been fighting from time to time, but no attempt at ethnic cleansing or genocide as such. While Kosovo was, at least initially, an internal Yugoslavian affair, Kashmir and Cyprus are international issues. In each, however, there is a strong cultural component.

For Kashmir, the roots of the controversy are more religious than territorial. A long history of Hindu-Muslim rivalry and conflict on the subcontinent underlies the bitterness and intractability of the dispute. The Pakistanis feel betrayed by the fact that the heartland of a predominantly Muslim region went to India during the 1947 partition that carved Pakistan out of formerly undivided India, and have continued ever since to regard fulfillment of their irredentist aspirations there as a primary national goal. The Indians firmly control the useful parts of the former princely state of Jammu and Kashmir and have no intention of leaving. They have told me many times, at many levels, that the integrity of India as a secular state, with a Hindu majority and a large Muslim minority, would be threatened if Kashmir went to Pakistan. Their argument may sound a bit contrived, but I am persuaded that many of them honestly believe that if Kashmir went to Pakistan, the old wounds of the partition days would be reopened and the continent as a whole would undergo another bloodbath. Whether or not that expectation is justified, the fact remains that the Kashmir problem has defied resolution for over half a century, and has provoked three wars between two large countries that have recently acquired a nuclear weapons capability.

The dispute over Cyprus is very different in detail, but here again we have two nation-states engaged in a protracted territorial dispute with no solution in sight. The intractability of the problem, like that of Kashmir, is based four-square on culture-bound differences. Greece and Turkey are each relatively mono-cultural and their two majority cultures have a history of conflict that goes far back. If it weren't for that residue of culture-bound antipathy, they could have worked out a permanent solution to their conflicting aspirations in Cyprus long ago.

The same can be said for many other conflicts between nation-states. Where there is no history of cultural conflict, solutions can usually be worked out, either bilaterally or with foreign intervention. Where there is such a conflict, solutions are much harder to reach.

It's a complicated world, with powerful cross-currents. On the one hand there are the trends toward transnational integration, which we shall discuss presently. On the other hand, a plethora of large and small groups of people who identify themselves as distinct societies are coming out of the woodwork and demanding that the world recognize their individual identities. Who are the people of East Timor anyway? What is their basis for nationhood? What about the Polisario, which is essentially a tribal confederation of Saharan nomads who have reorganized themselves as a "nation"? Should they have their own country or should they remain part of Morocco? How small can a country be and still have a seat in the United Nations? How big can a self-proclaimed nation be and still be denied that status?

A HAPPIER SCENE: CULTURAL MELTDOWN IN THE UNITED STATES

At the beginning of the twentieth century the United States was predominantly a monocultural society with a substantial black minority and an assortment of other minorities, consisting mostly of recent immigrants who had brought with them distinctive features of their various cultures. Profound demographic and attitudinal changes ensued that led us gradually to shed ethnic distinctions in some but not all aspects of daily life. Discrimination based on ethnic origins and race became less common in matters of religion, employment, and politics, and eventually such discrimination became publicly condemned and legally restrained. Ethnic and religious distinctions in such matters as marriage and place of residence eroded. National origins continued, however, as a source of pride for many individuals, who celebrated their provenance in innocuous ways like annual parades. Taking a very long view, during the twentieth century the United States went through an uneasy transition through multiculturalism toward becoming once again a monoculture—but of a new and different kind.

In 1986, a few months after I had retired and taken up my continuing affair with the Apple Macintosh, the phone rang. I picked it up, and the dulcet tones of an attractive-sounding female said: "Hi, this is Brenda, is this Carl?" My first instinct was to say "Brenda who?" but I restrained myself and just said "Oh," or something equally intelligent. Just as well, for it turned out that Brenda, despite the informality of her approach, was not in the least interested in identifying herself any further, or getting to know anything about me for that matter. She worked for a computer company, and was calling in response to my tele-phoned plea for technical assistance.

This started me thinking. When I was young, we used last names for business and for casual encounters, while first names were used for family and good friends. This was basic to how people treated each other. If I said, "Hi, call me Carl," I was mak-ing a friendly gesture, an offer of a closer relationship, more or less like offering a cigarette (another cultural artifact that has become extinct). What's going on? Was this business of rejecting surnames even for casual encounters a personal whim of Brenda's, or did it represent a basic change in the "common sense" that lubricates our society? I decided to check my data, in proper scientific fashion. The next time I called for technical assistance I just used my initials, C. S. Coon. Sure enough, eventually the young man who called back addressed me, throughout the conversation, as "C. S."

Well before Brenda called, I discovered that a radical change had occurred in my peer group's attitude toward ethnic jokes. This kind of humor has regaled and titillated culture-bound people all around the world since the beginning of history and probably long before that. The French and the English have been telling jokes about each other forever, and their lives would have been much drabber without them. Having lived most of my life in culture-bound societies, I appreciated this kind of humor and absorbed a certain capacity to play it back to others. And there had been plenty of that kind of humor in my own peer group, when I grew up. But now, telling an ethnic joke normally meets with shock and strong disapproval.

It eventually occurred to me that our society was going through a basic transformation in which many of the old values that once lubricated our interpersonal relations were being rejected. And those values were precisely the ones that identified individuals as belonging to one or another of the cultural subgroups that still make up our society. If your name was Art Nussbaum or Joe Stanislavski and you didn't want to be recognized as Jewish or Polish, you no longer had to change your name to Miller or Smith, you could just be known as Art or Joe. It made life simpler. Jokes that put down a specific ethnic group had been put off limits not only because they might offend somebody, but also because we didn't want to be reminded of our ethnic diversity. Meanwhile a special breed of ethnic organization flourished, designed to counterattack whenever it found ethnic slurs or discrimination against its group. Senators, congressmen, and other political leaders were biting the dust right, left, and center because of chance remarks that smacked of ethnicity. It all added up to a massive cultural attack against old-fashioned cultures.

Sometime after the Second World War, the United States of America decided to homogenize itself. It is well into the campaign by now with fair prospects of succeeding. But what is it gaining, and what is it losing, and how is it going to replace that which is being discarded?

THE MELTING POT: PLUSES AND MINUSES

I've previously postulated that when people move from one level of altruism, and the level of social complexity that it implies, to a more complex level, they don't lose the mind-set they started with, they simply graft a whole new set of attitudes and values on top. It's a matter of adding a new layer, rather than replacing something old with something new. Americans are adding a new worldview to their psychological repertoire, one that enables them to cope with the strains and contradictions that arise from becoming members of the larger group. We are moving away from an "us vs. them" mind-set based on being Yankees or Irish or Jews, to one of being citizens of the United States. It's like the transition I observed in that young Nepali hillsman who refused to divulge his caste, but on a grander scale.

As individuals, however, Americans still need that sense of belonging on the third level. We still need to belong to something that is bigger than the people we know personally but smaller than a subcontinental nation with over a quarter of a billion strangers in it. Most of us are still willing to talk about our cultural roots privately, but are uncomfortable when they are aired in public. But what else is available to satisfy that third-level need? What sort of third-level identity do we want to go public with? What kinds of labels, what kinds of social organizations exist that we can adhere to, in order to fill this gap?

If you look around, there are lots of organizations waiting to fill this need. First and foremost are the religious denominations. The percentage of Christians who still attend church regularly is much higher in the United States than in Britain and in Western Europe. Presumably the secular trend that has led so many people toward humanism and away from theism is based on arguments that are equally available in both regions. Can the difference be explained by the fact that Europeans still have cultural identities associated with their individual nationalities, that act as a cultural bridge between the second and fourth levels? And have correspondingly less felt need for the third-level sense of belonging that a religious denomination might fill?

Then there is politics. Join the Republican or the Democratic party, get involved at the grass-roots level, and share the sense of belonging to a larger community with like-minded neighbors. If party politics at the national level doesn't turn you on, then become politically active at the state or local level. The possibilities are quite varied.

Beyond all this there are many private organizations, ranging from philanthropic organizations and environmental activists, through professional and trade groups, to sport clubs and fitness centers. If none of the above suits, you can stay glued to your television set and root for your favorite pro football team.

Now the Internet opens up new possibilities for like-minded individuals to get together electronically and develop new organizations dedicated to everything from evolutionary theory to witchcraft, from stamp collecting to the study of memes. The problem appears to be that Americans face too many options, not too few. We're like the cow in the road, that went hungry although there was green grass on either side, because it couldn't decide which way to go. A great many of us are distressed, complaining of anomie, of a lack of sense of purpose. The closest thing available to fill that need is organized religion, but that is a wasting asset, not a rising star. Pro football doesn't really do the trick either, for most of us. Americans need a better solution.

THE REST OF THE WORLD

Every culture is different. Each is at least as different from all the others as each human being is different from everybody else. Cultures have personalities too.

Every country is different. Every one has its unique mix of geography and history, land and people. Some are virtually monocultural, some contain many cultures. Some have problems of assimilating newcomers from other cultural zones while others have problems of too many people and not enough resources. I could fill a book with nothing more than an explanation of ways in which countries differ.

Specific theories, applications, and approaches you may use to understand or deal with a given country won't work on a one-for-one basis in another country, even if that country is next door and looks the same from the outside. I have seen many foreign-aid programs squandering their resources trying to make water run uphill because someone in the donor agency had a global theory. There is no theory or approach or paradigm that works everywhere. We can observe that globalizing trends are putting everybody everywhere in a state of stress, and that culture-bound conflicts resist resolution, but beyond that we must be careful, and look at the world one piece at a time.

This situation is rough on theorists. If only somebody could invent a single approach to solving the world's problems that would work everywhere! But that hasn't happened, and it will not in the future. For those of us who like variety in life, that's probably all for the best.

NOTE

1. See chapter 7 of Thomas Friedman, *From Beirut to Damascus* (New York: Farrar Straus Giroux, 1989), for a graphic account of the Shatila massacre.

CHAPTER 13

COPING WITH CULTURAL DIVERSITY

I've talked about contemporary culture-based conflicts in Kosovo, Kashmir, and Cyprus, among other examples. Which paths should we take as we forge new approaches to eliminating old problems? Should our goal be a "final solution," in which local and regional cultural distinctions are eliminated entirely and replaced with a global monoculture? Is the only viable long-term future for humanity a uniformly light-brown population that takes its meals at fast-food outlets and meets its other needs at shopping malls? If so, if that is what most people are going to insist on having, so be it. But I don't think a species as curious, adaptable, and inventive as ours is going to settle for such a drab outcome. I am optimistic that the human landscape will remain varied and interesting.

151

Cultural diversity, to the world of the human mind, is analogous to what biodiversity is to the biophysical world. Both are in danger. The same forces that are decimating the tropical rain forests and destroying other habitats are planting fast-food emporia and shopping malls all over the world.

I grew up with cultural as well as biophysical diversity and regard present trends toward homogenizing everything with unmixed loathing. I like to visit faraway places and get off the beaten track and see people who are doing things differently, not for the tourist dollar, but because that's the way they always did them. When I went up to Kulu Valley over forty years ago and watched the gods come down from the neighboring villages for their annual jamboree, I rejoiced at the sight, although I was saddened by the knowledge that the custom was dying. Maybe it has been resurrected, for the tourist industry. If so, it won't be the same.

There's a great custom in Morocco called the "fantasia." It's a kind of hillbilly drag race, where Berbers come with their prize horses and flintlocks to a big village square. They collect at one end, then gallop as fast as they can to the other, and fire their guns in the air, with the horses rearing and snorting, and dust all around. I used to attend whenever I knew one was coming. But in the last few years, an enterprising Moroccan showman has built a big arena outside Marrakech, where horsemen do a kind of fantasia to the strains of the *Lawrence of Arabia* soundtrack blasted at a large audience of goggling Western tourists over a superpowerful sound system. In between the fantasia acts you can see belly dancers on camels and other exotica. Sorry, it isn't the same. What I saw was like watching wild animals in their habitat; what the tourists see is, at best, a zoo.

Maybe that's the only future for the marvelously diverse cultural quirks and customs that have always embellished the vast panorama of humanity: a human zoo, preserved in museums and theme parks, a kind of commercial virtual reality. But I wish it were otherwise. Does it have to be that way?

When I first visited Kathmandu I was visually overwhelmed by the carved facades on the old houses that lined the narrow streets there, and particularly in the neighboring town of Bhadgaon. Every house showed the handiwork of hundreds of hours of loving creative efforts by people who had lived and built there many generations earlier, when time was less important and beauty counted for more. When I came back in 1970, the facades in Kathmandu were mostly gone, replaced by dull concrete facades, but there were still quite a few in Bhadgaon. A young Newar saw me admiring them one day, and asked if I were interested in acquiring some of the carving myself. He told me he had recently inherited one such house and for a price that I could afford, he'd sell me the whole facade. I remonstrated: how could he divest himself of his inheritance in this way? I'll never forget his reply:

"You can afford to set a high value on this kind of thing. Your house has electricity and running water. My house does not. With the money you will pay me, I can install power and water. That's more important to me."

I didn't accept his offer. Much as I admired the product, I couldn't allow myself to participate in what seemed to me a kind of rape. But the facade soon vanished anyway, to be replaced by yet another faceless concrete wall.

This illustrates the core of the problem: Most people in most parts of the world want modernization and want it soon. They are tired of cooking rice on a dung-fired stove and going to the well for their water. Either they don't realize what costs they will bear in the modernization process, or they don't care. But the costs can be considerable. They can trade being a first-class

Newar, with a proud heritage and a solid cultural identity, for being a third-class, faceless member of a modern global society.

There are ways of resolving, or at least mitigating this dilemma. First, cultural artifacts can be preserved if they are seen to be important and funds are available. Philanthropic organizations could have provided funds to give my Newar friend his power and water in return for his agreement to preserve his old house facade. This has actually been done for some of the more picturesque temples and palaces, and by now the situation in Bhadgaon is more or less stabilized; much has been lost, but enough has been preserved to retain the essence.

Second, there can be a conscious effort to preserve the best of the culture. Too few modern political leaders have given priority to cultural continuity; one was Jawaharlal Nehru, India's first prime minister, who led his country from independence in 1947 until the mid-1960s. Nehru's genius rested in large measure on his ability to persuade his huge country that being an Indian was a good thing, that Indians should take pride in their cultural heritage, and that some things were worth doing simply because they maintained and strengthened cultural roots. Indians took the message to heart, and pride in being Indian has helped ever since to offset regional tensions and keep that sprawling giant of a country together. If India ultimately emerges from the current global cultural meltdown without the kind of major systemic breakdown I shall describe in chapter 17, then Panditji (as Nehru is affectionately known) can take much of the credit.

When I was in Nepal, I had to make a speech now and then about U.S. policy or some related topic. I would tell my Nepalese friends that I hoped they would lick their development problems, and we'd help where we could. I hoped they'd become a more democratic country, but it was up to them to figure out how to do it. But above all, I used to say, don't stop being Nepalese. Keep up your old ways wherever they don't get in the way of modernization. Preserve your traditions, your values, and your customs wherever you can. You'll be better off if you take pride in your roots, and the rest of the world will appreciate you more. I don't know how much impact these ideas had, but they were well received.

Every country with strong cultural traditions that is joining the modern global village must shed those attributes of its cultural heritage that create internal dissension or cause conflicts with its neighbors. But if, in the process, it extirpates its cultural identity entirely, except for what it preserves in a few museums, it will, in old-fashioned terms, have sold its soul for a mess of pottage. And all humanity will be the poorer.

Yes, culture has a future, for as far ahead as we can see, and probably a good bit farther. Especially the third-level culture, the kind that is still causing ethnic wars, religious controversy, and other growing pains. We need diversity in human cultures just as we need biodiversity. We need to aim for a global monoculture strong enough to prevent local wars, but not so strong as to turn us all into clones of each other.

CHAPTER 14

TOWARD A GLOBAL SOCIETY

If we have to settle on just one way to describe all the different changes that are shaking our contemporary world, we could do a lot worse than sum up our condition in one word: globalization. Culturally defined groups are no longer the prime vehicle for social evolution; multiculturalism is in, and the third level of altruism seems destined to become less and less relevant. Almost all the major problems humanity confronts these days seem to require international solutions, from ethnic cleansing and other local wars to drugs, refugees, and terrorism. Right now, as the new millennium begins, the web of multilateral and supranational economic institutions is rapidly thickening.

There is no master plan here, any more than there ever has been previously when humanity has struggled up onto a new plateau of complexity and efficiency. Each of us is adapting in small ways, and together all these small adaptations are building up, like a coral reef, into a new structure that will bind together societies all over the world.

ECONOMIC GLOBALIZATION

In the economic sphere we are in the middle of a massive, multi-faceted movement toward an integrated global economy.[1] The ways our largest corporations go about doing their business increasingly leap across national frontiers. Are our American corporations exporting jobs to cut costs? Are foreign interests buying and controlling some of the icons of our industry? Why should disturbances in the Asian financial markets affect the U.S. stock market? The internationalization of the U.S. economy is now felt by the average citizen. It is no longer the exclusive preserve of captains of industry, financial experts, and professional commentators.

POLITICAL INTEGRATION

The trend toward global political integration is also strong, but less visible. Loyalties are still primarily to the nation-state; support is limited for anything smacking of world government. Nations are reluctant to give up core elements of their sovereignty, but nevertheless they are sacrificing fringe elements of that sovereignty in order to allow international agencies to operate effectively in areas of strong national concern. International cooperation to control illegal narcotic traffic is one example. International courts to consider genocide is another. On the horizon: further nuclear arms control measures, further institutional arrangements to control the manufacture and distribution of chemical and biological weapons, and a strengthened international authority to adjudicate and control problems arising from refugees and migration issues. Humanity is thus inexorably moving toward conferring increasing authority on international groups, bodies, and organizations. And this is happening whether we like it or not.

For many people in the United States, the idea of world government is anathema. Some of our most prominent leaders, including figures in the United States Congress, publicly inveigh against the idea of world government in general, and against the United Nations in particular, with every bit as much enthusiasm as they used to inveigh against Communism and the "Evil Empire." To be pro-American in their view requires one to be opposed to the forces of international integration.

A sensible modern observer doesn't have to be either for or against world government as such. The forces impelling humanity toward integration are not going to be stopped by nationalistic rhetoric, any more than King Canute was able to stop the tide from coming in. The United States, as the surviving superpower, is well positioned to guide the way these forces play themselves out, so as to keep the process evolving along lines congenial to our American values and interests. Senator Jesse Helms and his ilk are doing our nation a profound disservice by getting underfoot and hindering our government as it undertakes to work with rather than oppose global trends. They may think they are the only true patriots, but history will surely judge them the opposite.

WHAT KIND OF WORLD GOVERNMENT WOULD BE CONGENIAL TO OUR INTERESTS?

As an American and a humanist, I profoundly hope that the global society of the future will be based four-square on the twin pillars of individual freedom and equality of opportunity. I hope that governments at all levels will be democratic, and that citizens will recognize their responsibility to keep them that way, as well as enjoying their benefits. This may sound like pie in the sky at the present moment, but it is the direction in which the most successful nation-states are leading the pack.

Then there is the question of what *kind* of democracy humanists would like to set as a goal for a future world order. Should power be concentrated at the center, or should it it be based on the federal principle, with layers of explicitly defined powers at various levels? My answer is a strong affirmative for the federal option.

There is a subtle but important correlation between the levels of altruism we explored early in this book and the federal principle. One's first loyalty is to one's family. One after another, layers are imposed on top of that basic loyalty: loyalty to the tribe, to the culturally defined community, and to the nation. Similarly, the basic element in the political spectrum should be the family. Then layers of government can be superimposed: county, provincial or state, and national. For each level except the most basic one the guiding principle is that of limitation of power. The powers of the federal government in the United States are expressly limited; other powers are left to the states. The powers of these constituent states are similarly limited, if not by law then by common consent, and residual authority resides in smaller, more local entities, such as counties and municipalities. This works fairly well, because it is consistent with our human natures. The problems every individual has in "working around" conflicts between, say, feeding the family and paying taxes, or between community loyalties and national patriotism, resemble the problems county and state and federal governments have in resolving jurisdictional issues that crop up between them. If we have succeeded so far in developing ever more complex societies, it is because in each case we have successfully managed to grow new layers and to learn how to manage them.

This principle of layers also applies to nongovernment organizations: big corporations, school boards, labor unions, political parties, and so forth. It has become ubiquitous in modern societies because it works better, both in producing results and in providing individual happiness, than the alternative of top-down control. Top-down authority doesn't work as well as layered authority because it goes against the grain of our human nature.

A future world government is more likely to be federal in nature if political globalization grows organically, step by step, rather than if it is imposed on some countries by others. That factor is in itself a strong argument for recommending a gradual approach to the idealists who are in favor of instituting world government as soon as possible. Furthermore, arrangements achieved gradually by consensus are likely to be more enduring than those achieved all at once by coercing major players into falling into line.

FUTURE INTERNATIONAL SECURITY ARRANGEMENTS

The situation is similar with regard to evolving international security arrangements. Here too the growth is incremental, and not always obvious. We can see some of the parts in place, while others are on the drawing boards, or being negotiated. Examples are the nonproliferation treaty, treaties limiting the nuclear arsenals of the major nuclear weapons states, and conventions prohibiting chemical and biological warfare.

I foresee the world community gradually moving in the direction of having a global police force, a regular army financed internationally and directed by the United Nations Security Council. It will differ from present peacekeeping operations in that it will be a standing force, available to move in when civil unrest inside a country becomes serious enough to threaten regional stability, or when mayhem of a genocidal nature threatens. The force would also be available to control brushfire wars between states that were sufficiently lacking in influence so that the infringement on their sovereignty would be something the UN Security Council could accept, and sufficiently limited in their military means so that the international force could readily control the situation.

This is not a recommendation, it is a prediction. The small wars that are constantly breaking out in various parts of the world these days are an increasing embarrassment to the leaders of the larger and richer countries. I see no other way out of the dilemma. Of course, if everyone in the world were to graduate at once, right now, to at least the fourth level of altruism, we would all be off the hook. But that is not going to happen. There will be more violence, not less, in the twenty-first century than there was in the twentieth. (More people, for one thing, plus the information explosion.)

As a former ambassador to Nepal, may I be permitted one parochial hope for that future international standing army? Let a significant share of the personnel, officers as well as troops, be from the Nepalese hills. The so-called Gurkhas are commonly considered to be among the toughest, most reliable soldiers in the world. The Nepalese hills are overpopulated and getting more so, leading to deforestation and other evils. The country is poor and needs the money. Policywise, Nepal is a master at getting along fairly well with everybody, except occasionally India. So for most of the world's trouble spots, use of forces from Nepal would be relatively noncontroversial. The Nepalese themselves are getting leery about sending their citizens to serve in other nations' armies, but would find their service in an international force to be acceptable, and even a source of pride.

CONCLUSION:
THE ROLE OF THE UNITED STATES

Given the present power configuration among nations, the United States is well positioned to have a strong influence on the whole process. If we are willing to recognize that we are heading into a situation in which we shall no longer, as Americans, have absolute control over our own destinies, we ought to be able to end up with a large degree of control over our own destinies and a solid ability to influence the destiny of all humanity. The key word here is "influence," as opposed to "control." In any future global society, everybody should be able to influence the course of events, but no one nation or faction or group—or ideology or religion—should be in control.

NOTE

1. For an interesting overview, see Thomas L. Friedman, *The Lexus and the Olive Tree: Understanding Globalization* (New York: Farrar, Straus, Giroux, 1999).

CHAPTER 15

POPULATION

O f all the things that have changed during my lifetime, the most pervasive and visible has been population growth. I revisit suburbs outside Boston where I spent my childhood and I am lost: the street pattern is totally different, and neat little quarter-acre lots stretch out where I used to play in the woods. I can't even find the place in Washington where my wife and I lived in 1950, when I first joined the Foreign Service. The site has been buried under a mall.

When I first visited Morocco, in 1939, the population was about 8 million, now it is over 30 million. Similarly with Nepal, which has grown from about 6 million (as far as anyone could tell at the time) to over 20 million. India in the late 1950s had about 400 million people; now it has about a billion. In the

United States the growth has been less, but the population has nevertheless doubled, since I was first old enough to understand numbers.

These figures come straight from my memory. Let's see how they check out with an authoritative source: "In 1950, world population stood at 2.5 billion. . . . Since then, world population has more than doubled, to 5.9 billion people. Now, about 86 million people are added to the world's population each year, with 98 percent of this increase occurring in the developing countries."[1] The world population passed the 6 billion mark in October 1999.

The global population explosion is, from a biological point of view, the most conspicuous of the many facets of the metamorphosis our species is going through. That does not, however, make it easy to understand. Human reproduction results from a very large number of individual decisions, and the factors affecting these decisions vary a great deal with place and time. A lot of experts have extrapolated global trends from limited databases, and have been proven wrong. Nevertheless, on a global scale the picture of what has been happening so far is clear enough. World population has exploded because death rates started to decline well before birth rates did.

Death rates dropped during most of the twentieth century. This is another way of saying people are living longer. The trend started in the richer, more technically advanced countries where modern medical techniques began and broad-based public health services were first instituted. Gradually these life-extending techniques spread throughout the world. By now almost (but not quite) everybody has at least limited access to them. Some of the worst killers have been eradicated (e.g., smallpox) or nearly so (e.g., polio).

Meanwhile, global birth rates continued at a high level. In

much of the world, before other economic development measures could take hold and appreciably improve living standards, children were still economic assets and a necessary hedge against old age. It was still "common sense" that it was a good idea to have a lot of children if you could. That kind of perception dies hard, and in many parts of the world it is still prevalent. There has, therefore, been an overhang period of at least two generations, during which global death rates were falling much more sharply than birth rates. By now birth rates are falling too, in most countries, but the damage has been done. In many countries, half the population may be adolescent or younger, and even if birth rates catch up completely with death rates, the population will continue to grow for another couple of generations. If the society in question is already straining the carrying capacity of the land, the pressures become enormous. The problem of cohorts—of having enough elders around to instill cultural continuity in the youth—becomes critical.

Birth rates are falling in most of the world because attitudes about reproduction are changing. Where the younger generation is better educated, public health facilities are available, and modern contraceptive techniques are at hand, people begin to limit the size of their families. Both parents come to realize that with one or two or at most three offspring, chances are good that their children will survive them. They appreciate the importance of educating those children, which costs money.

This attitudinal change has already begun to take hold in most of the developing countries. Demand for contraceptives now exceeds supply in some parts of the world. Problems continue, particularly in those countries that are lagging behind, but the overall trend is favorable. The problem is not so much whether as when. Nevertheless, time presses on, and the population bomb is still ticking.

COSTS OF THE POPULATION EXPLOSION

Environment: Population pressures, combined with modern consumption patterns, are the primary cause of pollution, destruction of habitat, deforestation, global warming, and other aspects of the environmental degradation that is currently concerning thoughtful people everywhere. Too many cars, too much energy consumption, too much demand for paper and other raw materials in the rich countries. In the poorer lands to the south, greenbelts and wildlife habitats are shrinking as farmers and commercial interests move in, while other people are swarming into shantytowns on the edges of new megalopolises, living in squalor, where they constitute breeding grounds for future unrest.

Economic development: Overpopulation impedes development in many of the poorer nations. This fact has been documented in many ways, by many observers. International agencies like the World Bank, government aid organizations, and a host of private philanthropic and research organizations all overwhelmingly agree. When too many people share limited resources, some of them get left out, or get very short shrift. And the state spends a lot of resources just keeping them alive, resources that are not paying the dividends in terms of economic development that they could pay if they were spent on investments aimed at economic growth.

Refugees: Directly or indirectly, population pressures exacerbate the growing global problem of refugees, and the related problems of migration that are increasingly bedeviling the more prosperous nations.

Crowding offends liberty: A dense population requires more constant and intrusive government intervention than does a population whose people have more space.

These are the most direct and obvious costs of the current global population problem. But there is an even more basic problem that the population explosion has raised, one of particular concern to humanists.

One of the most important specific humanist objectives is to bring about conditions in which every child born is wanted, is cared for, and is given a fair shot at making the most of its innate qualities. This condition may hold at present for quite a few children born in the richer countries, but in the poorer ones the prospect of the average newborn is bleak. Far too many of the children currently being born in the world as a whole are doomed to a life of poverty and ignorance; many are likely to die prematurely; only a few of the particularly gifted children being born in the poorest countries are going to "make it" into modern society and achieve the modern living standards that the rest of us take for granted.

This situation, from the humanist point of view, is intolerable. The quickest way out of it is to combine measures to improve education and raise living standards (economic development) with aggressive measures to effect a radical lowering of the birth rate in those areas and among those groups where the problem is most acute.

VOICES OF DISSENT

Not all observers agree with the foregoing analysis. The late Dr. Julian Simon, for example, was a vigorous advocate of the view that economic development alone would solve the problem, and as far as babies were concerned, the more the better. He attributed the unsatisfactory rate of economic development efforts in many countries not to overpopulation but to socialist and communist theories of government. Look at Hong Kong versus the rest of mainland China, or at South versus North Korea, he said. Simon noted that early warnings about the population explosion in the developing countries had focused on world food supplies and the threat of widespread famine as the number of mouths to be fed increased. Not so, he said; world food production actually increased faster than population.

Simon's point about food production once had some validity (it has less now), but he was wrong about almost everything else. His was a maverick view actuated by a right-wing abhorrence of anything smacking of socialism. His view that free enterprise alone would solve the problem of global poverty, regardless of how many people populated the planet, is, to the best of my knowledge, shared by very few.

A current dissent is based on the fact that in Europe, birth rates have fallen drastically in recent years, well below the replacement rate in many countries. In some countries (notably Italy and France) this has become a matter of national concern and governments are attempting to encourage more births through various fiscal incentives and social measures. To some observers this suggests that the problem for all humanity is no longer too many babies, it is rapidly becoming one of too few. Is the species heading for extinction? Is that the end result of the achievement of mass prosperity and universal access to modern contraception? The new doomsayers are full of gloomy analyses and predictions.

I am confident that prosperity does not require a lemming-like conclusion. We are a tough species with a strong survival instinct and we are not about to become extinct. Even if Europe were the only landmass in the world, and there were no developing countries with a problem of too many people, Europe's current population "implosion," as it is called these days in the press, should be regarded as part of the solution, rather than as another brand-new problem. We want every child born into the world to be wanted. What better way to achieve this goal than to achieve a balance between a society's need for more people, and their availability? Babies have been in oversupply for so long that we find it difficult to adjust to a situation where they are not. But surely what we are observing is a swing of the pendulum rather than a plunge into a form of mass suicide.

That is, of course, only part of the story. Europe does not exist in isolation. The Third World is producing many able people who will do everything they can to migrate to Europe and share its prosperity. But that, as we have noted, raises other problems and issues.

DEMOGRAPHIC HOPES AND REALITIES FOR THE DEVELOPING WORLD

The population boom in the Developing World is by no means a spent force. Birth rates are falling, but despite everybody's best efforts, global population will continue to increase for at least another two generations, probably longer.

For one thing, a population explosion as massive as the one we are now witnessing has its own momentum, for it alters the demographic structure of the population. When there are far more young people than old ones, the population will continue to increase, even if the number of live births per woman is tapering off.

Another major factor is that many countries remain culture-bound in a past that supports male domination and values large families. Several African countries, Pakistan, and Afghanistan are examples. These cultures are the stragglers, as humanity shoulders its way into the next millennium. They constitute unfinished business for the rest of us. We had best get that business over with as fast as we can, for the planetary clock is ticking.

In fact, we are all racing against time as we try to get the global population problem under control. The most important issue for the poorer and more overpopulated countries is not *whether* they will achieve some degree of balance between population and resources, but *how*. The choice is going to be between reducing their numbers humanely, through having fewer babies, or reducing those numbers brutally, through war, famine, and disease. If you think I am being overly dramatic, check out my detailed argument in chapter 17.

A FINAL THOUGHT

Recent technological advances are reducing the need for human labor. We can enjoy higher living standards without most of us being out in the fields or working on factory assembly lines; increasingly, machines do that kind of work. It follows that humanity doesn't need as many people as it used to, to provide the necessities of life. This doesn't mean that our numbers ought to shrink down to the minimum needed to run the machines; we'll need plenty of well-trained brains to do other things. But it does mean that the present global population is not only far too high in terms of its impact on the planetary support system, it is high in terms of what humanity as a whole needs to maintain our increasingly complex social structures and to continue to progress technologically.

There is no way for us now to determine what the optimum population of planet Earth should be a hundred or a thousand years from now. But we are headed in the direction of working it out, through a long and disputatious process of calibration. We know we have too many people in some areas, and we suspect that in some others we may be heading toward having too few. Patience, fellow humans. We're working on the problem. And we may even be making a little progress.

NOTE

1. *Population Today* (a publication of the Population Reference Bureau) 26, no. 3 (March 1998).

CHAPTER 16

ENVIRONMENTAL ISSUES

The future of our planetary habitat is being threatened by a synergistic combination of two quite different trends: the galloping global population increase, mostly in the Developing World, fueled by tradition, ignorance, increased food production, and successful public health systems; and galloping overconsumption, mostly in the rich, overdeveloped countries, which is inspired by old-fashioned capitalism and powered by the mass media. Either one of these trends would by itself constitute a major threat to humanity's future. Together, they are like the *two blades of a scissors*, slicing up the options that we ought to be leaving to our descendants.

It's easy to feel righteous and blame somebody else if you see only a part of the problem. Some intellectuals in the Developing

World blame capitalism and the former colonial powers for their continued poverty, which in most cases continues primarily because they have produced too many people. The rich countries fuss at the destruction of tropical forests and wildlife in the Developing World, and everybody is bothered by those aspects of global pollution that are clearly somebody else's responsibility. The air is full of indignant denials and pseudoscientific scurryings around, designed to demonstrate that the problem of the moment does not exist, or is in someone else's bailiwick.

In all this confusion, one thing should be clear, but isn't: *There is a balance of responsibilities between the poor overpopulated countries and the rich overdeveloped ones.* There is work for everyone. The poor countries have the primary responsibility to curtail their populations, as humanely as they can to be sure, but not too slowly, given the hot breath of the four horsemen on their necks. The rich countries bear primary responsibility for global pollution and the destruction of the earth's dwindling supply of nonrenewable resources; they must move as rapidly as possible to develop environmentally clean technology, to put it to work themselves, and to make it available to the poor countries. The rich countries also must help the poor countries every way they can to control population growth, and provide resources to help them make other hard choices when it comes to decisions that affect the planetary environment.[1]

All nations need to maintain a clear set of long-term goals. First and foremost is the preservation of the planetary support system. And that involves regeneration, bringing the planet back, as well as halting present destruction. Cost/benefit ratios are heavily involved—most of the steps we need to take to improve the environment involve measurable trade-offs, in the short run, against living standards. If you clean up the smoke emitted by coal-driven power plants you'll end up with a higher monthly electric bill. If you do away with nuclear power, as some environmentalists want, you'll end up with much higher electric bills, and probably brownouts to boot. These matters have to be negotiated, every step of the way, within each of the rich nations. And they will have to be negotiated between the rich and poor nations as well. No one wants to pay more than his share. The question resolves itself into a process for determining what the fair share for each party will be.

Such processes will have to buck strongly ingrained habit patterns. Traditional reasons for having large families remain powerful obstacles to controlling population in many countries. Less well recognized but equally intractable is a modern value system in the overdeveloped countries, led by the United States, that elevates consumption beyond the level of crass self-indulgence and makes it a positive virtue. Thus while the general direction is clear, getting mass support for the specific steps required will be enormously difficult.

The sine qua non in any such process is that all parties agree that the preservation of the planet is the most important single goal for humanity as a whole. When push comes to shove in specific cases, like preserving the tropical rain forests, this overriding objective has to take priority over tactical victories for individual groups. Such a consensus does not in itself provide the detailed answers negotiators must seek for individual environmental issues. But it is essential if such negotiations are to succeed in overcoming the severe attitudinal and political problems we face.

THE PAYOFF

One of the recurrent themes one hears in many developing countries is that the poor countries are poor because historically the Western powers have exploited them. Therefore, the argument runs, the rich must compensate the poor; foreign aid is not charity, it is like paying off a debt, or expiating an ancient guilt.

Indians and Algerians among others sang this melody throughout the Cold War era, as a sort of obligato to their major refrain of pious nonalignment. Now the Cold War is history, and the concept of nonalignment no longer makes sense, but the old leitmotif has by no means been abandoned. It has simply been dressed up in new terminology. The rich nations might as well brace themselves, for this old refrain's new words may well become the most argued single issue between the rich and the poor countries for the next several decades, or longer. It is a depressing thought, but when we think about it, the situation could easily be worse. The issues only start by involving high moral principles; they soon break down into subissues that are expressible in numbers, quantifiable and therefore amenable to negotiation and compromise. Ultimately we are not expiating a historic guilt, we are buying/selling a rug.

Technology can be expected to reduce at least some of the obstacles to negotiating future agreements on many of these issues. Take, for example, the industrial materials and processes that are currently causing pollution of the atmosphere and waterways. In many cases nonpolluting substitutes can be developed. If they are cheaper than the original materials or processes, the problem can be expected to go away in a few years, even without negotiations. Even if they are not, their costs can be expected to come down over time, to the point where their universal adoption becomes economically feasible.

Existing foreign aid programs are less effective than they ought to be, when it comes to helping the poorer countries introduce technological innovations of environmental importance. Each country and each culture is unique; to be effective, foreign aid must be tailored to local conditions. All too often, these programs have to conform to a "one-size-fits-all" approach crafted in the donor's head office back home. U.S. aid programs not only suffer from this approach, but are additionally handicapped in the family-planning field by domestic pressures.

The World Bank is working to slow the destruction of the Amazon basin's enormous forest expanses, the largest continuous green belt left on the planet. The arguments are many, but in this case it boils down to trading debt writeoffs for Brazilian restraint on the pioneers that are hacking and burning all over the basin. Surely this suggests a more general global pattern for the next several decades: Transfer of resources from rich to poor nations, to cushion the costs to the latter of cooperating in global efforts to preserve the environment. This isn't a question of who is to blame, and who should pay as a matter of equity; it is a matter of all humanity acting in its own best interests. Let the brahmins of both the developed and the developing worlds stop moralizing against each other. We all have to work together because we have only one planet between us. It's as simple as that.

Regional tensions often block even the most sensible environmental planning, and regional conflict can upset the applecart completely. A nuclear exchange between, for example, Israel and one or more neighbors, or between Pakistan and India, or India and China, could be a tragedy for the people immediately concerned. To what extent would it be a tragedy for humanity as a whole? Presumably the planet would not be rendered totally uninhabitable, as could have been the case after an all-out nuclear exchange between the United States and the Soviet Union. But given the problems for many countries that the meltdown at Chernobyl caused, who can assess the problems for the rest of us of even a relatively minor nuclear exchange in the Middle East or wherever?

A nuclear war is a worst-case scenario. There will be many other scenarios, many other problem areas, many other situations that could threaten efforts to make the planet more habitable and less dangerous. The high road to the future begins with efforts to convince as many people as possible that all humanity, not some narrower affiliation, is everybody's prime purpose. The situation in a sense is analogous to the difficulties the United States faced in earlier times, of reconciling regional interests. Even when such interests were sharply conflicting, the fact of being in the Union, and the perceived disadvantages of leaving it, overrode the local priorities. Except, of course, for our Civil War, which established the principle that the Union was not to be allowed to self-destruct because of differences between its constituent states. Do we have to go through a similar ordeal to convince the powers that be that the same principle now applies on a global scale?

NOTE

1. China is sui generis; it doesn't fit the "two blades of the scissors" analogy. It has taken radical steps to control its huge population but they may not suffice; a future relaxation of its population policies could have a devastating effect on global population predictions. It is still a relatively poor country but is close enough to technological modernity to have a huge and growing impact on global environmental problems.

CHAPTER 17

SOME PROBLEMS
OF THE POOR

India

F or all our progress, humans are still part of nature. We have now learned to influence and sometimes even control those parts of the natural environment with which we interact most intimately. But nature is always there, and if we fail to act, it takes over. Nowhere is this more strikingly evident than in some of the more overpopulated countries of the Developing World, where present population pressures are compounded by continued high birth rates to condemn whole cohorts of impoverished people to permanent underclass status. Either those countries take control of their population levels, and do it with compassion but effectively, or nature will do it for them, brutally. Somewhat arbitrarily, I have selected India as a case study for how the latter process might work.

India has achieved a great deal in the last fifty years. It has emerged as a large and economically powerful nation. There are several hundred million people in the modern sector. Out in the countryside, this includes millions of successful farmers and landowners who own most of the land, and who have embraced modern agricultural techniques with considerable success. In the towns and cities one finds many more people in government, industry, and other fields who are well educated and have enough income to enjoy at least an approximation of Western living standards and lifestyles. This class is growing rapidly. It is impossible to estimate how large it has become—for one thing, it depends on where you draw the line. But it does not yet constitute a majority. While this group was getting established, educating its children, building commerce and agriculture and industry, the total population of the country has grown, explosively, from about 300 million at the time of independence to nearly a billion. There are still hundreds of millions of very poor people in that overcrowded nation.

The impoverished half-billion or more Indians who are not part of modern society in terms of their economic status have, however, joined the modern world in another sense. The global information explosion has reached down into the villages and particularly into the urban shantytowns and informed everyone capable of watching a TV screen about the lives of the rich and famous, about the affluence that they are unable to share.

The raw facts are against these impoverished people, for there are too many of them for the nation's resource base to support. Imagine, if every one of them enjoyed an American standard of living: the whole subcontinent would be one big parking lot and shopping mall! Rich people take more space, consume more nonrenewable resources, cause more environmental damage than the very poor. Poor people cram together and the stink they make is mostly biodegradable. That is about the only known advantage of being poor, in the Indian context. India can support its present population only at the cost of most of them being poor. The only way the poor of India can become much better off is if there are fewer of them. But the population, alas, continues to grow at a frightening rate, despite energetic efforts by private agencies and government authorities to make family planning available to everyone. So the situation for the poor is bleak—and the difference between good government and bad government is not going to change that fundamental equation very much as far as they are concerned.

Try to imagine yourself in the position of an ambitious, upwardly mobile member of Bombay's semiskilled labor force. You are supporting a family on a pittance, working like the very devil, with no prospects whatsoever of a major improvement in your miserable living standards. You have access to the media, you see the lives of the rich and famous portrayed in vivid color every day, and you want a piece of it, but it's pretty obvious you aren't going to get it. Perhaps you'll relieve your frustration with a pilgrimage to a holy place, and meditation; or perhaps you'll turn into a philanthropist and help the even needier; but it is also quite possible that you will nurse an incubus of rage and frustration, which sits in you and festers for years, as you look down the tunnel of your future and see no spark of light. Someone comes along and says it isn't hopeless, or it wouldn't be except for the fact that some neighboring group[1] is doing you in, and maybe you find that easier to accept than the notion that your only real enemy is a massive demographic bulge. Many of the people we are talking about would rather do something, anything, than just sit around passively and suffocate by inches. Enter demonstrations, denunciations, demagoguery, and eventually intergroup mayhem.

Now let us move on to the next stage of the argument: over time, there is increasing public disorder and violence between groups, accompanied by a diminishing sense of social responsibility, except that solidarity *within* these groups continues to rise. This kind of disorder has always occurred sporadically in parts of India, so much so that it can be considered endemic. The question is whether, given growing population pressures, particularly in the cities, it will continue to increase and become even more widespread. If that happens, what will be the manifestations and the consequences as the pressure increases and surpasses anything experienced so far?

Many Westerners have prophesied the disintegration of India over the past five decades and have been proven wrong. India has staggered along in its unique and wonderful way and has made significant progress. But this albatross of a restless, underemployed underclass has continued to grow. I don't know whether we are talking in a time frame of five years or fifty, but it does seem likely that if something does not happen to shrink this underclass substantially, and fairly soon, then it will eventually erupt in disturbances that will shake the nation and even the world. Let us look at a possible scenario:

The capacity of organized government at all levels to suppress disorder and even to provide essential services becomes increasingly stressed. We are talking about a continuum here, not a single sharply defined boundary. Eventually the point is reached where lawlessness and violence are so widespread as to be virtually the norm in large parts of the country, and essential services in those regions break down. *Then* the horsemen of the Apocalypse—war, famine, and plague—reappear on the scene, just when modern men and women, with all their new technology and their humanitarian instincts, thought they had banished them for good.

Item: Not only are the police unable to cope with armed insurrections, and the army unwilling, but organized armed forces of government at various levels start fighting each other. It has happened in India, on a small scale; and with the example of how Yugoslavia disintegrated, who can say India will never experience conditions tantamount to civil war? And as we know from our own experience, civil wars can be very bloody.

Item: If civil authority should collapse in a major region, would the Indian railway system be able to serve it? And if a local crop failure should hit that area, who would get the food in from national reserves, and from abroad, and how? We have the example of the Sudan, and there are far more people at risk in, say, the Indian state of Bihar, than in the Sudanese southland.

Item: What happens to public health facilities in an area where civil unrest has taken over? And what happens to epidemics when health authorities are prevented from getting at the victims?

I am not predicting how soon any of these crises might arrive on the Indian scene; in fact, I am far from certain that all or even any of them will necessarily happen in India at all. It's quite possible that if they do happen, they will occur sporadically and infrequently, handled as temporary emergencies that do not threaten the integrity of the nation.

I am, however, reasonably certain that somewhere in the world this kind of scenario is going to happen, and most likely it will happen over and over again in various places during the coming several decades. The combination of an impoverished underclass condemned to permanent penury and an information explosion that shows it how others live is combustible. If your house fills with gas, it may still not explode until someone lights a match. I cannot tell you who is going to light the match, or when and where, but we should all be warned: there is a lot of combustibility building up in the poorest parts of the world, and it will get worse before it starts to get better.

NOTE

1. In the Indian context we are talking first and foremost about religious communities, especially Muslim versus Hindu. Within the Hindu majority we are talking about subcastes. In poor overpopulated regions elsewhere, loyalties may be organized along different fracture lines. The point is that regardless of region and local circumstances, we are talking about culturally identified groups at the third level of altruism, as defined in chapter 6.

CHAPTER 18

SOME PROBLEMS
OF THE RICH

The United States

Every country and every culturally defined society is unique, with its own particular set of attitudes, problems, and potentials. It follows that there are limits to the applicability of the global theories I am expounding in any specific national or cultural context. I picked India as my subject in the last chapter because it has the largest number of desperately poor people living under one flag, which makes it important in its own right, and in the hope that some of the features of the Indian scene have at least a limited relevance elsewhere. In the same spirit, I shall look at the United States now, because it is important in its own right, and some of its structural problems will be found, to some extent, as existing elsewhere.

RAMPANT CONSUMERISM

Capitalism has been enormously successful and has done extra-ordinary things for human progress, but there is a cyclical principle at work here: its drawbacks are becoming more evident to more people, and the pendulum is probably starting to swing against it.

In the nineteenth and early twentieth centuries, capitalism led to monopoly and the stifling of the competitive principle that was its lifeblood. In the United States, we learned to control that problem. More recently we have seen that capitalism leads to an emphasis on persuading the public to consume at unhealthy levels. We have yet to learn to control that tendency.

In the 1920s production outstripped consumption and by the 1930s we found ourselves mired in the depths of a Great Depression. The Second World War in a sense rescued capitalism from this dilemma by sharply increasing the requirements for goods and services. After the war, some Americans sensed the need for a drastic increase in public consumption patterns, if a balance between production and consumption was to be maintained and another great depression avoided. The hucksters and ad men who had always occupied a niche in our society proliferated and gained great prestige (as well as material wealth). Many of our great institutions of learning, like Harvard, replaced traditional areas of study, like geography, with courses in motivational research and disciplines like "Human Relations" and "Social Dynamics." Television came in, providing an ideal new medium for the deployment of the "hidden persuaders" that the new disciplines in academe were developing. America's romance with the big, gas-guzzling automobile took off, aided by enormous investment in the interstate highway system, providing both a huge new market of its own, and a mobility that allowed shopping malls and theme parks to proliferate.

Ideologically, the emphasis was not only on encouraging the public to overspend on new goods and services, but on making people "feel good" when doing so. TV programming, with its sitcoms and talk shows, was a key instrument in turning the moral virtues of frugality and saving upside down. As the shopping malls and big chain stores took over and virtually wiped out the mom-and-pop stores, they became the central places of a new ethos of hedonistic self-gratification, the new cathedrals to which the adherents of the new lifestyle flocked.

As a child I was taught to acquire material things sparingly, and to use up the things I had before I replaced them: "Use it up, wear it out, make it do, or do without!" How old-fashioned that sounds these days!

The modern capitalist lifestyle, based on consuming even when it means running into debt, is beginning to run aground on its own contradictions. The most telling signs are in the environmental field. The present level and types of consumption in the United Sates cannot be sustained indefinitely without seriously impacting the environmental support system on which all life depends. We have cut back on fluorocarbons, we are trying with some success to control the automotive and industrial emissions that are seriously polluting the atmosphere, we are considering more drastic pollution-control measures to head off the threat of global warming, and we are moving fairly energetically to protect endangered species and certain natural habitats. All of these measures and more are being opposed by the more old-fashioned capitalist "bottom-liners," but public opinion, supported by the more enlightened industry leaders, is in favor of change.

I take it as axiomatic that the very concept of progress must be redefined to include greater emphasis on conservation of planetary resources, even if it entails some reduction in living standards. This can and should entail a redefinition of moral values, not necessarily returning to the old ones I was taught as a child, but a new and better synthesis.

WHO CONTROLS THE ELECTIONS?

There is a relationship between rampant consumerism and the mass media that bears watching, particularly in the United States. The more successful producers of goods and services have learned how to persuade the public to buy their products whether that public needs them or not. The basic technique is advertising, particularly on television. Increasingly in recent years, the people seeking national power have learned to mimic this approach in seeking to gain elective office, as a first step toward imposing their own agendas.

During 1998 and 1999, the Republican Party in Congress tried to impeach President Clinton. The hard core of the attackers was a group of conservative white males who were going for the president's jugular because they hated what he stood for. They are the losers in an ongoing redistribution of power in this country in favor of blacks, women, recent immigrants, and other groups who until recently have been outside the power structure trying to get in. These losers remained undeterred by the fact that their ostensible reasons for the impeachment effort had nothing to do with how the president had been doing his job. More to the point, they remained undeterred by compelling evidence that the majority of the American people wished they would quit. In other words, we were witness to a flagrant violation of the democratic principles on which our country depends for its continued existence as a constitutional democracy. The effort failed, but it succeeded enough to demonstrate the clout of a determined minority, when that minority is well financed.

Proposals to reform the way election campaigns are financed pit the well-heeled few against the many. Their failure to get off the ground, at least as of this writing, constitutes a serious systemic failure of our American constitutional democracy, perhaps the most serious in recent decades.

WHO CONTROLS THE MEDIA?

The failure of the impeachment effort demonstrated that democracy is still alive and well in the United States. However, underlying trends continue that could threaten the fundamental principle of majority rule, which is the essence of democracy and the sine qua non of personal liberty. The country could face, in short, a reversion to tyranny.

If it happens, it will be a new kind of tyranny, based not on raw power as such but on control of the media. The majority of the American public is hooked on television and has yet to develop a healthy resistance to TV advertising. The many billions of dollars that keep television afloat come mainly from advertisers peddling their wares. The fact that these funds continue to flow attests to their effectiveness; informed by a mentality devoted to the bottom line, industry would soon find out if its ads weren't working, and shift to other means to sell products and services. All well and good, our society can survive this, though it does distort our consumption habits and contribute to the pattern of rampant consumerism.

The more serious threat is that an oligarchy may emerge that can control the flow of information to the public. The trend is in this direction. The giants of the information industry are following the more general corporate trend and are seeking mergers, the better to compete in the world market for their products. These giants don't yet constitute a monopoly that controls everything; there are still plenty of alternative sources of information for those who care to seek them out. We still have a free press, and the Internet is turning out to be an unruly brash adolescent in the media world that appears for now to be irrepressible. But the trend gives cause for concern.

Everyone who believes in liberty and democracy should vigorously resist any and all efforts, however disguised, to control freedom of speech and the press. As much as in the days of the founding fathers, free speech and a free press is the ultimate guarantor against tyranny. Lose it, and we could lose everything.

THE HAVES AND HAVE-NOTS

One of the great unresolved issues of our time, and especially within the United States and other prosperous, well-developed countries, is where to draw the line between humanitarian concern for less advantaged individuals, and the needs for society as a whole to develop its economic strength. Do we level up or level down? If we invest enough in helping the poor and disadvantaged, do we stultify the economic growth we need to provide for future generations? If we emphasize growth do we neglect the neediest among us? Where, in short, should we put our priorities? The issue is being debated in one form or another throughout much of the world. It mirrors on the domestic scene the issue of the great disparities of wealth and economic development between nations. It is an ideological argument, and advocates of each extreme are equally passionate.

My childhood roughly coincided with Franklin Roosevelt's New Deal. One of the first books I remember reading was Hendrik Willem van Loon's *An Elephant Up a Tree*. Masked as a children's book, it was a biting satire on capitalist America in the Roaring Twenties. I still carry around the image I first gained from it of people pouring big containers of milk into the Hudson while down in the city children were going hungry. I read a lot of books when I was a child, and this image was amplified by many others. It seemed to me that I had narrowly missed growing up in an era of rampant capitalism, where getting rich equated to virtue, and devil take the hindmost. FDR may not have been the savior, but he certainly applied a massive course correction. Big, paternalistic government was in.

It has taken most of my life, but now at last we have returned to an era where the zeitgeist of rampant capitalism has regained respectability. It commands a majority in the Congress, where the dominant Republicans are going around with wrecking bars, demolishing a goodly portion of the social safety net established under FDR and his successors. The *Washington Post* and the *New York Times*, bastions of liberalism, sound as though the Turks were once again at the gates of Vienna, threatening destruction of the whole civilized world. But they are not the only, or even the dominant, voices in the media hubbub that are clamoring for the public's attention. You get what you pay for, and the rampant capitalists are paying copiously to get their messages across to the public—and of course to as many legislators as possible.

Don't get me wrong, I am not a flaming liberal. I see many things inside those gates of Vienna that deserve to be torn down. Liberalism has had a multigenerational opportunity to show its stuff, and while it has accomplished much of value, it has made mistakes as well. Perhaps the present Republican Congress represents a course correction that is needed in much the same way that FDR's was. Perhaps we see here a kind of bipolar principle at work—a dialectic type, in that the thesis (rampant capitalism) led to the antithesis (New Deal liberalism), which is now leading to a synthesis, which will hopefully incorporate some of the more successful features of both its predecessors, while avoiding some of the more egregious foolishness. That synthesis will necessarily, however, prove inadequate to meet the needs of rapidly changing times, and will therefore become a new thesis, which will provoke reactions leading to a new antithesis, and so on.

"Rampant capitalism" and "New Deal liberalism" describe historical conditions out of which we have emerged. We are not going to repeat exactly the same cycle, next time around. It seems to me that if there is indeed a bipolar principle at work here, we ought to be able to identify the extreme points of the oscillation in a way that is less tightly identified with the current historical context. Let's therefore examine each of the two poles in some detail.

The Republicans now dismantling much of the New Deal's bureaucratic legacy are commonly considered to be conservatives. But that is an oversimplification. There are two main schools of thought within the party. The Christian Coalition, which has achieved a more commanding position within the organization than its numbers justify, is motivated primarily by a fanatical devotion to traditional Christian values. Its membership is unabashedly conservative. But when we look at the more moderate, business-oriented wing of the party, I think it fair to consider many of them as proponents of rapid progress. Much of their fiscal philosophy is aimed at freeing up venture capital and encouraging growth in production. They are broadly internationalist in their view of the rest of the world. Their progressiveness is flawed, and largely obscured, by the fact that many of them are relatively insensitive to environmental concerns, which have to be central to any contemporary definition of progress. But this is due more to a single-minded, old-fashioned attachment to the so-called bottom line and to corporate profits as a means toward greater production than to any ideological aversion to the conservation ethic and principles. If and when the present lot of younger capitalists grow up, the majority can be expected to become good conservationists. Indeed, some of them already are. The essential point here is that as between their concern for the plight of the common man and the challenge to get on with whatever it is that constitutes progress, it is the latter that has their fervent support.

The contemporary American liberal is more concerned with social justice than with the bottom line. He or she sees increased profits for the few not as a means of stimulating investment but as something mildly obscene, particularly when the poor are getting poorer and the middle class is barely holding its own. Unemployment constitutes a failure of the system, not the individual. High profits should be sacrificed to the goal of distributive justice. Fairness is important, and if the rich are getting much more out of the national product than the poor, there is something fundamentally flawed with our society. The typical American liberal, in sum, is a humanitarian rather than a progressive.

Like the Republicans, the Democratic Party's message has lost its clarity. While Republican Luddites have been outshouting and outmaneuvering their moderate wing, the Democrats have moved toward the center. So it is a Democratic president who is the true progressive these days, trying to guide global trends toward growth of an international structure of agreements and commitments congenial to future American interests, and a Republican Congress that has been doing its best to block him at every turn.

Just imagine how much simpler it would be for the American voter to sort out the issues and decide on basic directions, if the choice were between avowedly progressive and clearly humanitarian parties! Of course there would be a myriad of issues to talk about, but they could be placed in the context of a clearly defined framework that everyone understood.

Maybe we have something like that already, though the context is muddled. If we step back from the details, hasn't American society as a whole operated for many generations under a general bipolar principle, oscillating slowly between emphasis on its progressive impulses and its humanitarian ones? Only episodically and relatively briefly have matters gone to extremes, as with FDR's New Deal and as with the current Republican Congress. The more normal condition is somewhere in between, with the national impulse aimed at working out solutions to current problems that represent compromises somewhere along the less extreme portions of the spectrum.

I believe that this tension between the two extremes, and the slow oscillation between them, is largely responsible for our huge and extraordinary success as a nation. We see a problem and devise a solution. When it doesn't work, or works only imperfectly, we sense whether it is too progressive or too humanitarian and adjust its position on the spectrum accordingly. We do not, of course, articulate what we are doing in these terms; it is a matter of common sense, that is, the prevailing balance of commonly held perceptions, expressing itself through the democratic process. Countries that don't have this kind of bipolarity, or lack democratic institutions, get stuck for long periods of time with solutions to prevalent problems that are either outdated or extreme, and suffer.

This ever-evolving dialectic between our progressive instincts and our humanitarianism provides much of the philosophical basis for my personal philosophy, which I call *Progressive Humanism*. It is like the balance of powers principle that undergirds the United States Constitution, and keeps the U.S. government from going off the rails completely. When new problems arise, the nation tries, through protracted debate, to strike a reasonable balance between solving them (progress) but in a humanitarian way (humanism).

CHAPTER 19

FAMILY VALUES

Women and men have been partners forever, from the beginning. We need each other, and always have, for the simplest and most cogent of all possible reasons: the survival of our species through the propagation and rearing of our successors.

If we could replicate ourselves like amoeba we never would have made it to our present state. Because of bisexuality, each person is created as a blend of the genetic material of two other distinct individuals. The resulting uniqueness of each individual is what has given our species the flexibility to survive and prosper. It expedited the process of evolution through genetic selection during our early development; and it has been equally effective, more recently, in terms of our cultural evolution.

This mutual dependence, of men on women and of women

on men, is among the most ancient and enduring features of our human condition. It is not, however, one of the most stable. Gender relationships have changed in the past, sometimes radically. They are inordinately sensitive to cultural variations, and indeed the ways they work themselves out in specific cultures can be considered hallmarks and defining characteristics of a culture. At present they are going through a radical transformation, particularly in the West, where they are integrally related to the many other radical changes I have been discussing.

This chapter is a sequel to chapter 10, "A Woman's Place." I shall discuss changes now underway in gender relations and speculate as to where they may be headed. The discussion will be limited to North America and Western Europe, because this is where the cutting edge is slicing farthest and deepest into traditions. There is a lot going on in other countries, regions, and cultures as well, and much to be said, but there are limits to what can be covered in a work of this scope.

KINDER KUECHE KIRCHE
(CHILDREN, KITCHEN, CHURCH)

The old German summary of the proper role for women has been blasted sky-high by the introduction and widespread use of contraception, which has done more than anything else to make the gender revolution possible. Before contraception, women were the prisoners of their biology. There were limits to how far they could go beyond their traditional roles in the nursery, the kitchen, and the church without renouncing their biological roles as mothers, and risking social disapproval.

Now a woman no longer has to choose between being a mother and having a career; she can do both, if she has the strength, and be a role model to boot. This is an extraordinary 180-degree turn in the most basic factor underlying male-female relations, and it has come about for the most part in living memory.

The introduction of contraception has not, of course, guaranteed women equality in the workplace. They are still handicapped by the fact that they have to take time out from a paying job to have a baby, and the process of rearing the child also falls more heavily on the mother than the father, at least during infancy. There is a perceptible effort at present to work out arrangements that moderate this handicap, such as maternity leave (sometimes for men as well as women), prekindergarten schools, and nurseries, along with a growing consensus that the father needs to contribute a more equal share to the time-consuming aspects of parenting. But the basic problem continues. A recent survey indicates that the most highly stressed sector of our population is young working mothers.

The working woman also faces a well-publicized problem in the job market, that of equal pay with men, and equal opportunities for advancement to the higher ranks. Older men still control the senior-level positions in almost all sectors of the economy, including law, finance, medicine, engineering, and many other fields. They want to maintain this control, not because they are misogynists, but because it is what they were brought up to expect. The battle has been joined, but it is still far from being won. There is still a glass ceiling and it is still important. Women have battles ahead of them, but it is a generational thing, and seen in a generational context they are well on their way to transforming society. There is no turning back: the men who oppose them now are going to retire pretty soon, and their replacements will be different.

GENERATIONAL SHIFT IN ATTITUDES

During the last twenty or thirty years, I have dealt with entry-level Foreign Service officers, with Peace Corps volunteers, and with students on various campuses. I have been consistently impressed by the vitality and competence of the young women in these groups, women who are destined to take on many of the jobs and responsibilities that would have gone almost exclusively to men when I was younger. The gender revolution has clearly unleashed an enormous reserve of energy that social values had kept bottled up for many generations.

Older women, in the West at least, have been through an extraordinary wringer, a convulsive about-face between the roles they were taught to aspire to as children (being a good wife, mother, and homemaker), and the wider opportunities that have opened up for them more recently. Many of them, I suspect, nurse inner conflicts between their aspirations and their upbringing. It is not an easy transition for them. Better off are the younger women, who begin on the crest of the wave, less encumbered with self-doubt and, in many cases, guilt.

As for the men, the older ones for the most part are resigned or resentful or both. You can always get a laugh with a "dumb blonde" joke, but you had best not tell it where women will hear you or you will be in trouble. These older men display a general attitude of dyspeptic resignation that rather reminds me of German attitudes back in 1946, when I was a young American soldier in Bremen. The prevailing attitude there was, well, we lost the war, we lost it fair and square, we'll suffer through the next few years, and maybe things will get better, though I guess they'll never be the same as they used to be.

The younger men haven't had to adapt to the new situation,

they were born into it, and accept gender equality as a natural part of life. It's a fine example of the plasticity of our species, a cultural about-face in an important aspect of culturally dictated behavior, accomplished within the scant period of about a generation and a half.

ON COURTSHIP, MARRIAGE, AND MALE PATERNAL INVESTMENT

There has been a sea change in the West, in our lifetimes, in our attitude toward sex. Young people engage in sex before marriage without arousing the righteous indignation such behavior occasioned in the past. It is even considered sensible and proper, in many circles, for a couple contemplating a lifetime commitment to live together in a protracted state of premarital bliss, checking out the validity and durability of their relationship. Often they marry only when they decide the time has come to have a child. Is this wrong? Is this immoral? Only by the ethical standards we inherited from an era that preceded contraception.

In terms of present-day realities, the sex act has been decoupled from marriage and procreation to a considerable degree. What has replaced it as the central pillar of marriage is, in my view, an updated version of that ancient criterion, male paternal investment. Small children have an atavistic and enduring need to have both a father and a mother intimately involved in their growth. If a man and a woman have a baby, and the man vanishes over the horizon, he is acting in a way that is immoral not just by Victorian standards, but by modern ones as well. This helps us perceive what I think is only now coming into focus as the basis for a new modern morality about sex and marriage. Paternal obligations are already codified in our laws. Society's traditional disapproval of the delinquent father is growing stronger, at a time when most of our other inherited dos and don'ts are losing their old force. To be sure, the woman contemplating marriage and procreation still has much the same problem as the one that bedeviled her Paleolithic ancestress, namely that of judging whether the man she plans to marry is sincere and will stay the course, or if he is only interested in sowing his oats, and will flee when the going gets rough. But modern women can and should be able to count on social sanctions to back up their judgment. Modern men should be constrained in their instinctive impulse to spread their genes as widely as possible by these same social sanctions.

Divorce is a tricky issue, but this concept of the importance of male paternal investment sheds some light on it. Divorce between childless couples should carry less of a legal burden of liability and a moral burden of guilt than divorce that occurs during the child-rearing stage. Isn't this what the stress on "family values" is all about? The key point is to give children a break, let them grow up as part of a family, more or less as their ancestors did, for thousands of generations.

Modern society hasn't resolved the issue of how the working mother can be fully competitive in the job market when she is also trying to bring up children. More emphasis on the parenting responsibilities of the father can help, but even if the father shares fully 50 percent of the child-rearing burden, this still leaves the working mother (as well as her husband, in this case) at a competitive disadvantage, vis-à-vis the unmarried or childless individual who may be competing for the same job.

MORE COMPLICATIONS

What constitutes maternity in an age when one woman's egg can be fertilized in vitro, and carried to term and delivered by another woman, or when a gay couple adopts a child? What constitutes paternity, when so many single women are raising children on their own; when serial divorces and remarriages confuse the issue of which child belongs to which father; when in vitro fertilization at least theoretically permits a woman to carry a child of unknown parentage; when a lesbian couple adopts a baby?

What about the statistically prominent issue of the single mother, who may or may not have been married at one time to the father of her children? How can society permit this woman reasonable freedom of choice, including the right to remain unmarried, and still give the kids the environment we think they need?

How about gay and lesbian marriages? Are children growing up in such unions disadvantaged? If so, and if it can be proven, should such couples be denied the right to adopt children? What if one of the partners brings children to the union? and so on . . .

Some of these anomalous conditions have come about because of the relentless forward march of the biological sciences, that now give us capabilities to control human reproduction unknown to earlier generations. And some reflect changes in the way adults, especially women, regard themselves and their social roles. Women want jobs and a status in the workplace equal to men. Gays and lesbians want equal rights as well. Old-fashioned family structures are being challenged by new possibilities, all of which are happening at least somewhere, furnishing grist for the media, while some people applaud and others watch with fear and loathing.

It isn't enough to be a Luddite. Going back to old-fashioned family values simply is not going to work. We can't put the technological genie back in the bottle. And who are we going to authorize to decide to which of the various sets of old-fashioned values we should revert? How about the Taliban in Afghanistan; does any American, even the most far-out member of the Christian right, want to adopt *their* system?

It seems to me that what is needed at the moment is a heightened concern for the child. I know I am being repetitious, but the point needs repeating: humanists want children to be born into this world only when they are wanted, and only when they have a reasonable prospect of being allowed to develop their innate capacities. If it can be demonstrated that a family headed by a mother and a father gives a child the best chance to grow up successfully, that gives us one kind of directional signal. If it can be further demonstrated that children benefit from having siblings in their immediate family as they are growing up, that gives us another signal.

Our society has partly succeeded in breaking the link between being the biological father and being the male in the family that helps bring up the kids. Stepfathers may or may not do the male paternal investment thing as well as biological fathers; presumably that depends on personalities and other circumstances. There is little doubt, however, that they do play a useful role when the biological father is dead, or has absconded, or is off raising some other woman's family.

We have had divorce as a normal and generally accepted way of resolving husband-wife tensions for upward of three generations now. With each new generation we get a little closer to the notion that the father-figure is the man in the house, whether that man is a biological parent himself or not. It makes a lot of sense as long as your society has a lot of divorce and remarriage. If you don't like the trend, logically you should oppose divorce in principle, although that seems like a losing stance in this day and age.

Separating a person's genetic role from his or her familial one resolves or at least eases some of the problems society now confronts. It cuts down the confusion and static for all con- cerned, including the children, when a divorced person with children remarries. It takes the sting out of some of the issues I raised regarding in vitro fertilization. But it doesn't resolve everything. For example, what is a judge to decide in a divorce case when the father is responsible and competent and wants equal custodial rights? Is he as entitled to them as the mother? Should he be required to remarry? What if he is a closet gay and ends up with a male partner? Clearly, there are some rough edges remaining here.

And finally there is the issue of whether the kids have a right to grow up with siblings. We have too many people in the world and cutting back to a more sustainable level requires cutting back on families. Does this mean aiming for a large number of one-child families? Or could it mean simply having fewer par- ents, each couple having several children? The latter is at least equally feasible arithmetically.

One can postulate, for example, a culture in which most people did not reproduce, but those who did have children would have large families, five or six or more. The expectation would be that on the average only one or two of those offspring would themselves reproduce. The rest would be aunts and uncles. They would maintain close relations with their nephews and nieces, sharing in some aspects of parenting, but their primary contribu- tions to human progress would lie in fields other than parenting.

The African wild dog (*Lycaon Pictus*) follows this principle, and apparently has managed quite well with it for the last five million years or so. The *Science Times* (section C of the *New York Times*) of December 3, 1996, gives a fascinating account of the social life of this unusual carnivore: "Only one pair of dogs reproduces in a pack, and the rest of the adults relinquish parenthood to serve as babysitters, nannies, and even wet-nurses for the alpha pair's pups." The pack, numbering up to twenty dogs, is socially cohesive. "Aggression is muted in the wild dog . . . they hardly fight at all, and they don't even bare their teeth at each other."

CONCLUSIONS

This analysis raises many questions and provides few answers. Perhaps it is too soon to know the answers. If so, it would seem prudent to encourage diversity in the coming century or two, as different people and different cultures find their own ways to achieve domestic relationships that provide for enough reproduction but not too much, and for individual freedom but not at the expense of the children. Let a hundred flowers bloom, and let the ones that work out best for all concerned be the models for the generations that follow.

Should we therefore aim for a global society where nobody is under any peer-group pressures whatsoever, where every individual or pair of individuals is completely free to work out family relationships as she or he pleases? On the face of it this is an attractive prospect, but I have reservations. Human beings are social animals. The constraints, as well as benefits, of living in a social group have been part of our makeup ever since our origin as a species. Our goal, in my opinion, should be a society that provides substantial freedom of choice, but also provides some moral and ethical standards, and some peer-group pressures to conform to "commonsense" norms.

It seems to me that future generations are more likely to find such a balance under conditions of cultural diversity. Every culture establishes standards for matters relating to marriage and procreation, and those standards help mediate between the often conflicting interests of the individual and the social group. The problem in the past has been that if, for example, you were born into a society that insisted on child marriage, you were stuck with it. If there is more intercultural mobility in the future, this problem could be reduced.

Perhaps this is the best answer we have as we peer into an uncertain future: Maintain cultural diversity regarding family values, and let individuals select where they want to be when they settle down into a familial relationship. If anyone wants to offer a more specific long-term solution to the question of future family values, let that person do so. I have neither the clarity of vision, nor the courage, to do the job myself.

A FINAL THOUGHT

The sense of partnership that ought to provide the basis for relations between the sexes was distorted and suppressed during the past epoch of male domination. Now that women are asserting themselves, it would be useful for all of us to remind ourselves that male love for female, and vice versa, is the sine qua non of human existence. But it will take time to unlearn old habits of thinking. Some of the women who have been leading the charge for equal rights have assumed adversarial roles, in opposition to the males who dominate the workplaces and power centers they want to move into. The search for a new sense of what it means to be a woman has sometimes had the effect of diminishing female esteem for the opposite gender while provoking an opposite reaction from men.

Gender relations are exceptionally fluid at present. The people who are alive today, especially the ones in the affluent Western countries, are forging new standards of what is correct and acceptable. I hope that coming generations will be inspired not by adversarial relations between the sexes, but by an enduring respect for the fact of our total and permanent mutual dependence.

CHAPTER 20

PHILOSOPHY AND THE ARTS

REVOLTING INTELLECTUALS

In other chapters I have discussed radical changes that have been taking place, during our lifetime, in international and domestic political and economic relations, in lifestyles and habits of consumption, and in gender and family relationships. Truly tectonic upheavals, all of them; our nineteenth-century forebears, if brought back to life today, would think they were on another planet.

Similar upheavals have taken place in philosophy and in the arts. The most creative thinkers in each of these fields have been on the cutting edge of efforts to make sense of the massive technological changes being crammed down the throat of an unready humanity. It is these thinkers, more than the presidents, popes, and CEOs, who have led the effort to forge new frames. But that has always been the case.

They began their effort early. While most of the rest of our grandparents were still feeling at ease with the frames of the Victorian era, intellectuals like Martin Heidegger, James Joyce, Arnold Schoenberg, and Pablo Picasso were beginning to twitch. Each in his or her own way sensed that everything was coming unglued and the world was out of kilter; somehow the human juggernaut was careening down the highway to the future at ever-increasing speeds, and nobody was in control.

By the mid-twenties the German philosopher Heidegger was announcing that all the old philosophers had been asking the wrong questions. Jean-Paul Sartre and others followed, introducing existentialism and other philosophical schools to an already confused public. Schoenberg led the most progressive composers to atonality, producing music which may have been inspired, and it certainly reflected the confusion of the times—but it didn't sound like music at all to most of the concert-going public. James Joyce wrote *Ulysses* and *Finnegans Wake*, which almost nobody could read, let alone understand, but which everyone talked about. Picasso turned the old rules of painting on their head. And so forth.

There are two ways of looking at this revolt of the intellectuals. From the outside, from the viewpoint of the general public, they had for the most part simply taken leave of their senses. They hadn't just taken a sharp turn away from classical traditions, they had flat-out rejected them, and had emigrated to a world of their own. A pox on them, said the general public. We'll listen to Stravinsky and Debussy, and admire the paintings of Van Gogh and Monet, that's modern enough for us.

The intellectuals saw themselves in a different role. They

were building on the past but saw so much in the present that was out of kilter with the times that they considered it essential to throw out most of the intellectual baggage that still cluttered up the thinking of their contemporaries. They weren't moving to an entirely new house, as the rest of the world thought, they were trying to refurnish the old one, and get it into shape for the tasks that lay ahead. If they sounded confused to observers who sat outside their own circle, well, the times were confused, and the observers ought to be trying harder to get the message.

The rest of us never did get the message, at least not in its original form, which tended to be highly confusing, whether or not you consider it to have been inherently confused. What has happened is a synthesis, a coming together, between contemporary intellectuals and the public. There are at least two dimensions to this evolution.

The public has come, for the most part, to accept that many of the beliefs that Victorians held to be axiomatic are no longer valid, or at least are open to question. There has been a general clearing-out of the old furniture of our minds.

And both in philosophy and the arts, there has been a massive trend toward globalization. The patronizing "orientalism" through which Europeans once regarded non-Western cultures has given up a lot of ground, and is even on the verge of becoming politically incorrect. There is much more attention these days to Buddhist and other non-Western schools of thought. Non-Western musical structures are invading the classical music of the West, while Western popular music has invaded every other part of the world.

This strikes me as being a part of a larger pattern. Are the contours and character of that pattern becoming a little clearer?

POST-POSTMODERNISM

What basic assumptions will undergird future creative thinking? What philosophical structures seem most likely to take over as the current postmodern fads fade away? What will be the basis for the next millennium's "meta-narrative"? These are bold questions, and any attempt to answer them is hazardous. However, if the current trends I have been describing continue, then probably much of the serious thinking during the next millennium is likely to be based on the following:

- Humanism, in one form or another, will replace the old religions.
- Evolutionary theories will completely replace creationism and increasingly provide the operating principles for both historical and current analysis and comment.
- A new spirit of universality will increasingly infuse art, science, and philosophy. Schools of thought based on culturally or geographically defined units will be relegated to niches and lose importance.
- True gender equality will be achieved, with profound ripple effects on social values and attitudes.

These new structures will not be perfect, but they will be more compatible with what we know about ourselves and our planet than the modernized holdovers of the old structures now fading from the scene. They may not endure forever but I predict that during the next century, in one form or another, they will come to dominate the thinking of our descendants.

One reason we have a hard time peering only a few decades into the future is that the landscape is still littered with the wreckage of the attitudes we inherited. My experience in Bremen, Germany, in 1946 comes to mind. I was drafted into the U.S. Army at the very end of the Second World War and sent to Germany the following January. Bremen was a rubble of blasted buildings, all laid waste except for a few historic buildings at the center and a few suburbs on the periphery. Everywhere you looked, Germans were hauling bricks away from the rubble and stacking them in neat piles in designated places. They were thin, for the most part, and often hungry.

But what a change took place in only a few years! As they cleaned up the mess they reconciled themselves to the fact that they had well and truly lost the war. In the process, they jettisoned their old ideas of race superiority and world domination. Many of the young people started to think of themselves as Europeans first, Germans second. Currency reform came along and the German economic "miracle" blossomed.

The upheaval we recently experienced in philosophy and art reduced the assumptions and philosophies of our predecessors to a rubble that is at least as total as the physical destruction was in Bremen in 1946. But Bremen was soon restored, new and better than ever. Could something similar happen to our global society as we pick our way through the present litter of discredited ideas and frameworks? The global miracle of reconstruction will not happen as fast as the postwar German reconstruction did, because the scale is larger and the issues less clear. But to the extent our leaders are inspired by a new vision of the future, and show that they can in fact lead, the reconstruction could proceed faster than we might think possible. Unfortunately, that is a very big "if." If by contrast we continue to muddle along, it will take a lot longer to clear away the rubble and get on with the job of creating the first truly postmodern global society.

CHAPTER 21

FROM RELIGION TO HUMANISM

Religion still plays an important role in most of the world's cultures, but how important is it, or should it be? The answers are as diverse as the cultures themselves. On this issue as with others, I must limit the geographic scope of my analysis. I shall focus on the United States, because it is both big and interesting.

Conflict continues within the American body politic between atheists at one end of the spectrum and the fundamentalist Christian Right at the other. Most Americans subscribe to views that fall somewhere in between. Those at the center of this spectrum, probably a majority, don't go to church very often though they were brought up to; they believe in both God and evolution; they support both the constitutional separation of church and state and the motto "In God We Trust"; and they wish that a certain background buzzing of cognitive dissonance would go away, but know deep down that it won't.

The continued political clout of the Christian Right is a source of both puzzlement and concern. How can their leaders continue to assert that God created the world 6,000 years ago? Nobody else in the United States pays attention when they assert this kind of literalist nonsense, so why don't we all get together and put them on some kind of a reservation where they can preach to each other and leave the business of sorting out our problems to the rest of us? Why let them continue to stand up in our national legislature and on school boards throughout the country and get in the way? When will they figure out that they are not our moral and ethical keepers, they are simply a minority with a worldview with which nobody else agrees?

There are grounds for hoping the problem will wither away fairly soon. When you're on the backside of an evolutionary trend that is as profound and rapid as this one, you eventually change or at least become irrelevant. And yet, the old religious persuasions, the ones that held our ancestors in thrall, continue to have remarkable staying power. If they are on their way out, they certainly don't show it.

The answer is that the religions of our forefathers meet different kinds of basic human needs. In some ways these old faiths have gotten out of joint with the times and are more trouble than they are worth, but in other ways they seem to be just as necessary for human comfort and solace as ever. That's why many middle-of-the-road Americans still insist that they believe in God even though they no longer go to church. Let's hark back to our earlier systemic analysis of religion, reexamine its components one by one, and try to separate the disposable from the essential.

STRUCTURAL BELIEFS

Fundamentalist Christians take the Bible as the literal truth. God in His heaven, Jesus the Savior, the Creation myth, the whole ball of wax—they really believe it all happened. To the rest of us, these people may appear as credulous as the man who bought the Brooklyn Bridge, but they come from a long and honorable tradition. Not too many generations ago, most people in the Christian world shared their convictions, because they helped provide the semblance of an understanding of the nature of humankind and the cosmos at a time when there was little scientific evidence of a contradictory nature.

Many if not most practicing Christians these days don't believe all those myths and fables to be literal, historical truth; but they are willing to accept them as useful, in that they add color and coherence to their preferred system of religious practices and moral codes. Nonfundamentalist theists play along, in other words, and tolerate the earnest protestations of the true believers, the way adults tolerate children's faith in Santa Claus.

I cannot believe that the fundamentalists' propensity to believe in the literal truth of the scriptures will long endure in this modern age. We no longer have to invent reasons why we are here or who and what we are, for we have scientifically validated explanations. Darwin has replaced Genesis. The creationists are fighting a vigorous rear-guard action but their stand cannot prevail forever.

Humanists are right to challenge creationist theories wherever they raise their heads. We can confidently stand up for science and oppose superstition everywhere, and especially in our schools. Whatever atavistic need the old theories addressed can be provided better by the modern equivalent.

The same thing cannot be said, however, for the issue of whether God exists, as opposed to whether everything in the Bible has actually happened. God is a multifaceted invention of the human mind, and serves several important purposes. Get rid of Noah or Moses or even Jesus Christ himself, and a lot of people will still need God. For these individuals, God satisfies a strong emotional need for an enduring relationship; he is someone who will always be there, someone to turn to in times of stress, someone to talk to when no one else is available. You can jettison the whole of the creationist dogma, and subscribe fully to the scientific alternatives, and still want to believe in God.

This is a difficult problem for the humanist who rejects the idea of God, and even more for the atheist who vigorously opposes it. How to cope with the modern, scientifically sophisticated believer? My own instinct is to be tolerant and patient. Nonbelievers can and should work with scientific believers on a wide range of tough issues humanity faces, from saving the planet's ecology to abolishing conflict and restructuring society along more humane lines. Perhaps, as we approach closer to the ideal of a genuinely humane global society, there will be fewer individuals needing a deity they can relate to directly. And if that doesn't happen, who cares?

NARRATIVES

Every religion has its stories, its fables, its gospels, its origin myths. They combine details of everyday life with explanations that extend and exemplify the structural beliefs. They are a powerful aid in instructing children.

This is an easy thing to modernize. Let our schools take the best narratives from *all* religions and expose the toddlers to the whole mélange. As the kids grow older and realize what they have learned, they will internalize the oneness of all humanity, and gain useful perspectives on the kinds of religion their own society has graduated from.

This, incidentally, is another good reason for preserving the separation of church and state. As long as there is a strong secular tradition in our nation's public schools, no one faith can insist on monopolizing the curriculum with its own narrative material.

RITUAL

Ritual acts, events, and celebrations are repetitive events that support specific religions in a variety of ways. As a general policy, humanists and atheists alike should seek out ways to support existing rituals that are secular, start new ones, and graft new meanings onto old ones. Volumes could be written on this subject. Here are a few suggestions.

Holidays: Religions, like nation-states, often celebrate the birth anniversaries of their heroes. (Less commonly, religions like Shi'a Islam celebrate the deaths of their martyrs.) Maybe in the fullness of time the world will celebrate the birthday of Darwin. But in the meantime, humanists and atheists can and should emphasize the secular aspects of existing holidays, attaching new meanings where possible to old annual events— or at least recalling the pre-Christian origin of some of them, like Christmas. Other approaches might include special events, perhaps connected with ecological efforts like mass tree-plantings, to be held over as much of the world as possible.

Music: The world will wait a long time before the humanist family produces geniuses of the caliber of Bach and Beethoven.

Bach's B minor Mass and Beethoven's Missa Solemnis rank among the greatest pieces of music ever composed. They will continue to be played and loved long after the old religions have withered away. And why not?

There is a considerable body of Christian hymns sung at Sunday services. Must this go by the boards? Not if modern men and women compose new secular lyrics for the most popular old hymn tunes, to be used in the more advanced churches, and on public occasions where religious-type music is expected. This is a good example of how new meanings can be grafted onto old messages, easing the transition to modern times for that majority of any population in any culture who are comfortable with the familiar and instinctively resist change.

I could go on at some length with further examples from art and literature, festive events, and rites of passage, but I simply cannot provide a detailed road map in a book of this breadth. Suffice it to say that this whole subject of developing new humanist rituals opens up extraordinarily wide opportunities and challenges for human creativity.

CODES OF CONDUCT

This may well be where traditional religions are most susceptible to modernizing influences, and where it is most important that humanists be alert to the possibilities for change. The fundamentalists, who still insist on literal acceptance of the old structural beliefs, currently insist that they hold the high moral ground, and that the erosion of support for religious doctrine, as they espouse it, is responsible for the social disintegration and confusion they see around them. Nonbelievers should work with those believers who have rejected the old structural beliefs while retaining a belief in the existence of God. Both groups are likely to be distressed at current social trends, and can, to mutual advantage, cooperate toward creating new ethical guidelines out of contemporary chaos. They should, while seeking positive answers to new ethical issues, firmly oppose fundamentalist efforts to infiltrate and dominate our public educational system, for it is essential that the youngest members of our society learn at an early age that there are sensible modern solutions to contemporary ethical problems.

And finally, we need leaders with a sense of drama. Gandhi and Martin Luther King Jr. knew how to take current problems and dramatize them, wrap them into larger questions, and force people to think about their ramifications. We need issues that force a reluctant public to confront the fact that some of the ideas and assumptions they grew up with are out of date and must be changed. We need leaders who can take the fundamentalists on and demonstrate how dysfunctional their dogmatic views have become.

We cannot afford simply to sit back and wait for the fundamentalist spirit to die out, and for everyone to graduate to that fifth level of altruism on their own. That will take too long, for many of the problems discussed in the last several chapters are urgent, and cry out for enlightened, purposeful policies and actions. We need enlightened, modern leadership, and we need it now.

That leaves us with one final question: should nontheist humanists seek to discredit the old religions completely, in order to clear the way for more modern ways of thinking, or should the old religions be encouraged to evolve into new forms that retain some of the old roots, while replacing or at least updating some of the more dysfunctional aspects of their beliefs and practices? In an ideal world several hundred years from now, should there still be substantial numbers of people who identify themselves as Christians or Muslims or Jews? Or should everybody be a humanist or atheist of some kind or another?

The answer, in my opinion, is that the old religions need to evolve and become increasingly informed by a humanist perspective. As this happens, the need felt by many individuals to have faith in something inherently unknowable can be redirected and channeled toward positive modern goals. Instead of obstructing the process of coming out of humanity's cocoon, and adding to the pain, those who prefer to remain believers can be part of the solution. If such individuals prefer to continue to identify themselves as Christians or Muslims or whatever, it won't really matter.

CHAPTER 22

RACES AND RACISM

R aces exist. They exist because we are biological organisms resulting from the same evolutionary principles that produced all the other animals and plants that grace our planet. Even before we became fully human, our ancestors inhabited environments that differed widely in such matters as climate, topography, latitude, and proximity to bodies of water. Racial differences are the result of natural selection over countless generations for suitability to conditions determined by these kinds of variables.

The contemporary humanist may well ask, is race a good thing or a pain in the neck? It certainly qualifies as bad when it reinforces cultural divisions and thereby encourages intergroup violence. But it is part of our heritage, it is part of how we got to

225

be the way we are. Like the sex drive and the urge to kill, it is part of our roots. We need to recognize it, try to see whatever good we can in it, build on it, improve it, and become stronger and wiser as a result.

THE FUTURE OF RACES

Races are like God: a distinguished past, a wobbly present, and a highly uncertain future. Humanists and many others now realize that it is time to dispense with the idea that God will provide. Similarly, most of us are more sophisticated than we used to be about race problems, and some of us can foresee a time when race will no longer be a divisive factor in human relations.

Do we foresee, as some of my more thoughtful friends claim, that race problems will go away sometime in the future, but only as and when our species achieves a homogenized, coffee-colored uniformity? Is this what we want? Or should we assume a different scenario, in which for a very long time to come we shall remain diverse in our physical features, continuing to bear testament to the multiplicity of experiences of our ancestors?

I suggest that this issue is not a very important one, compared to some of the other issues I would like us to ponder now, as we develop the frames we need for an uncertain future. I would like all marriages henceforth to be successful ones, in the sense that children will only be born when wanted, and the father will stay on board and help raise them. If an interracial marriage meets these criteria, fine. By and large, marriages between individuals separated by a wide gap in upbringing have less chance of succeeding than marriages between individuals brought up in much the same way, but this is not an absolute. So the question of the future of race answers itself. If

there are enough successful interracial marriages over the next dozen or so generations to homogenize us, well and good. If not, that is all right too, provided we can learn to bury ancient racially based animosities. There can be strength in diversity, particularly when it is such an integral part of our roots.

RACE PREJUDICE

We've noted the trend in many parts of the world toward multicultural societies, where formerly distinct cultures are being dissolved in larger, fourth-level nations. Once a society becomes multicultural, there is a natural tendency toward it becoming interracial as well. A few states like Brazil and some of the Caribbean countries have been multiracial throughout their modern history. The United States, traditionally populated mainly by Caucasian immigrants from Europe, is also a frontrunner. In California, African Americans, Asian Americans, and Hispanics have already gained a majority between them, or are about to. In European countries, new underclasses are forming of immigrants from North Africa, Turkey, and other regions. Their numbers are increasing and subtle processes of assimilation are imperceptibly eroding former racial homogeneity.

All this mixing is not without pain. All of us, even the panhumanists who ascribe to the fifth level of altruism, still have that third level lurking within us; we still feel more loyal to our own group than to outsiders. The politics of increasing racial diversity leading to assimilation plays itself out differently in every country, but everywhere, the route is complicated and the way is full of potholes.

Assimilation is like a bowl of punch at a party. You can blend in different elements and it can work pretty well. But not if someone comes along and throws in something that doesn't belong there, like an old shoe or a dead cat. The dead cat in our American punchbowl at present is the general concept that some races are more intelligent and able than others. This idea has led to such a painful situation that it is often politically incorrect even to discuss the subject of race, unless for the purpose of condemning "racism." We have reacted to the presence of the dead cat by choosing to deny that it exists. Unfortunately, that hasn't made the punch taste any better.

My own views on this treacherous subject can be summed up as follows: there are physiological differences between different racial groups; we know that, we can see some of them. Does this extend to behavior? We don't know, and probably never will until it becomes politically correct for nonpartisan groups to conduct objective studies of that aspect of human nature. But even if such studies should show that racial differences of a behavioral nature exist, *it doesn't matter*! Behavioral differences abound within each racial group, after all. We are all members of the same species, we are all on the same team, and what matters is our own individual talents and capabilities, not the particular race we happen to spring from. Every race has individuals who are particularly talented in one way or another; no race has a monopoly on anything that matters in the realm of human capabilities.

The modern humanist overrides atavistic race prejudice and associates with other individuals according to whatever criteria are important to him or her—criteria that emphatically reject racial stereotypes.

CHAPTER 23

TECHNOLOGY IN THE TWENTY-FIRST CENTURY

Oh sage, can you see
By the dawn's early light
What you proudly proclaimed
In the dark of the night?

As anyone who has tried it knows, predicting what is going to happen is a lot more chancy than analyzing what has already happened. Take technology. The next crucially important technological breakthrough is likely to come when an individual or a small group, beavering away like tens of thousands of other researchers, puts something together with what someone else is doing in some other place. These people are so far out on the edge of human knowledge that most of us don't have a clue what they are up to. How then can we armchair pundits sit back and say what the next breakthrough will be? Anyone who could do this should not be writing a book, he or she should be playing the stock market and getting rich.

There are of course exceptions. Astronomical events can usually be predicted with a high degree of accuracy. Most of the events that people or groups plan to hold in the near future actually come to pass and can therefore be predicted with reasonable assurance. Demographic trends can now be forecasted with some assurance, at least in the short term. So can the weather. Specific events are harder to predict: riots, assassinations, political and strategic crises in general. The stock market, and economic affairs in general, are about equally hard to predict.

The most difficult issues to predict are those that depend on the interaction of several dimensions of human activity. What are the broad outlines of the course humanity, propelled by technology and demographic pressures, is taking as it careens, rudderless, into the future? Can you add the knowable, like next year's population increase, together with a whole lot of unknowable factors, like next year's assassinations and terrorist attacks, and come up with something knowable? I doubt it. And if you cannot even do it for next year, how can you expect to do it over the longer term?

The task of predicting the future is even more difficult in the present era than it customarily has been in the past. During this century humanity has managed to increase the complexity of both its material culture and its sociopolitical structures to an unprecedented degree. This section of the book, therefore, takes only a few very general stabs at predictions. It dwells mostly on what I believe humanity is capable of achieving if enough people have a clear vision of what our curious, inventive, adaptable species can accomplish.

A COMPUTER-DRIVEN WORLD

We've had enough recent experience with our new digital world to know that it is too useful to abandon; indeed, we cannot even sit still. We are going to keep on getting faster and smarter mechanical extensions of our brain, both for the home and for everything else.

Computers and robotic devices have drastically reduced the human labor required for production. Computers, scanners, and bar codes have made it easier for merchandisers to provide goods and services promptly while maintaining minimal inventories. First malls, and now the Internet, have made it easier for consumers to buy what they think they need. These factors alone go a long way toward explaining the sustained growth of the American economy during the last decade of the twentieth century.

The emerging global economy is both dependent on the growing capability to process complex data instantly, and a prime factor in seeing to it that our data-processing capabilities continue to improve. The same can be said of government, education, scientific research, and virtually every other field of human enterprise. What this all adds up to is that we are going to be more capable in the future than ever before to achieve whatever material goal we set for ourselves rapidly and economically. And that capability is increasing by leaps and bounds.

ENERGY

We can predict at least the possibility of a comparable breakthrough on the energy front. The next big leap may well be fusion power, and it may start to come sooner than most of us now expect. We have more than one approach that shows promise. "At present, the Z machine can produce about 20 percent of the energy, 40 percent of the power, and 33 to 50 percent of the temperature required for nuclear fusion to produce more energy than it consumes."[1] We humans are pretty good at tinkering with machinery to improve that kind of statistic. When we get this far down the road, it's probably a matter not of whether, but when.

Even if it takes another century or two to accomplish, when we have fusion power we shall have taken a leap forward of a magnitude that equals the discovery of fire. There will be no more electric bills, except perhaps a small charge for operating the facility. Petroleum will be for lubricants not fuel. The end of smog will be in sight. Interplanetary travel will become much more feasible. When energy becomes almost as available as air and water is now, all the equations governing our relationship to our planet will be affected.

BIOTECHNOLOGY

If the last decade of the twentieth century comes to be known as the era of the information explosion, the first decade or two of the twenty-first century is likely to be witness to a comparable explosion in biotechnology. There are already so many recent breakthroughs, and they cover so many areas, that one hardly knows where to begin.

Crop production, including organic pest control, and food preservation are just the beginning. Cloning, dramatized recently by the sheep Dolly, builds on a long line of other breakthroughs, but it is by no means an end in itself. We are chipping away at deciphering the human genome and already have progressed far enough to enable us to perform what any other age would have considered miracles. Organ transplants are already with us, a commonplace, and will soon be followed by the development of other animal species as "factories" for the production of such transplants. We can examine the genetic code of a human fetus for genetically transmitted disease and in some cases correct it. We can hybridize different species, producing chimeras (watch out, there may soon be a mermaid after all!). And we have yet to discover limits; we are still in the first stage of exploring an unknown continent.

It seems reasonably certain that over the next century our successors will have to cope seriously with the issue of human longevity. Not immortality, but a capability to extend the average human lifespan to perhaps double its present period. The treatments to accomplish this will be expensive at first, and someone will have to decide who gets them. The rich countries will have them first, raising other issues and concerns. Social attitudes and policies will be profoundly affected. In short, we will be launched on a course that will make us a different kind of animal.

This list is not comprehensive; there is no way it could be. It should be noted, however, that all these potential developments, and many others, will be related. Each of them will have ripple effects that stimulate the others. There is a vast synergy at work here, and from where I sit it appears unstoppable. Right as we watch, the butterfly is dropping out of its cocoon.

NOTE

1. *Science News* 153 (January 17, 1998): 47. The Z machine is an accelerator at the Sandia National Laboratories in Albuquerque, New Mexico.

CHAPTER 24

ISSUES FOR A FUTURE GLOBAL SOCIETY

The other day I was walking up a steep and rocky trail in the Blue Ridge foothills near my house. The footing was tricky, and required me to twist and turn abruptly, almost every step or two, to obtain solid footing and avoid a tumble. I found myself automatically looking ahead as I raised each foot, and if I was going to turn at the next step I would turn my foot while it was still in midair, so that when I put my weight on it my body would automatically be pointed in the new direction. I recalled that this was a trick I had learned half a lifetime ago, when I was wandering around the mountains of Northwestern Iran with a Shahsevan guide we called "Best Guide." He was a great guide and a superb mountaineer, and though I was a lot younger, he led me a merry chase through that rugged terrain. I used to follow right behind him and put my feet exactly where his had just been. Up until then my practice had been to put my feet down in the exact direction I had been following, then twist my body as needed. It was more work that way, and less secure. I learned my lesson by literally following in his footsteps, and absorbed it until it became second nature.

Change the scale by several orders of magnitude and you have a parallel with what we are discussing here. If your vision of the future is limited to the next step only, you will work harder at struggling up the trail, and your footing will be less secure than if you look ahead a little farther and select the footing you choose for your next step accordingly.

Let us make the hopeful assumption that in another couple of centuries, the humanists have taken over, population is receding, vegetation is advancing, the ozone hole has closed, God is a subject of only historic interest, and the global village is establishing its computer-driven dendriles over the face of Earth. What kinds of issues or problems will our descendants then face? What questions will they be asking? What kind of a future will they be defining as they set their goals for even more distant successes?

1. How can the global village best govern itself? Where should the balance be struck between the needs of the individual and the needs of society as a whole? Where is the optimum balance between local and regional autonomy on the one hand, and the need for a consistent approach to problems of a global nature?

2. What about social justice? Should our descendants assume that whatever utopian condition we eventually arrive at, there will always be richer and poorer people, and some will always be powerful while others are weak? Or should the aim be total equality? Or should it be something in between, some new synthesis that still, as I write, remains unformulated?

3. Should public policy encourage all cultures and all racial groups to merge into a single homogenized population, or is it important to preserve at least some aspects of present diversity? Will efforts to achieve global agreement on ethical standards that eliminate war, achieve population balance, and ensure a respect for universal human rights require the end of human diversity? What will humanity lose if diversity disappears? How best can we achieve humanity's goals while preserving diversity?

4. How can we reconcile individual choice in reproduction issues with the needs of the whole society for a total population that is in balance with our needs and with the environment's carrying capacity? How can we determine how many people is enough, and how many is too much? Should each culture decide this issue for itself, its decision influenced by both the global community and local cultural and political factors?

5. What kind of planetary environment do we want to create as a legacy for our descendants? Should we seek to undo the ravages humanity inflicted on Earth in the past, and restore it as much as we can to its prior condition? Or should we aim for some kind of Garden of Eden? How much control do we want to assert over natural evolutionary processes? Will we want to experiment with genetically engineered life-forms?

6. What general limits, if any, will we want to impose on genetic engineering as it affects our own species? Where should we draw the line? Should we strive for maximizing the longevity of the individual human life? Can we predict how that would effect the essence of human nature and human society?

7. We shall of course be pressing outward into space. Why? And what will our priorities be for space exploration as compared with our terran objectives? (This will be heavily influenced by what we find out there. Eventually we shall probably

discover signs of extraterrestrial life, possibly even of intelligent life).

The above outline just scratches the surface. The most important point for future generations will always be: can we and will we keep on asking such basic questions? Can we and will we maintain a vision of the future that gives our present condition a sense of direction?

CHAPTER 25

GETTING FROM HERE TO THERE

Progressive Humanism

There is no way that anyone alive on the planet today can tell the rest of us exactly how we must navigate in order to bring humanity out of its present chaotic state to a calmer, more unified, more purposeful condition. It would be almost as realistic to expect a caterpillar to tell an emerging new butterfly what to do next. But there are a few observations that can and should be made.

If we cannot expect existing authority to give us precise answers to the many specific questions that are constantly popping up, what *should* we be looking for by way of general guidance? Are there general principles we can agree on? Are there conceptual frameworks that can help us think more clearly about the choices that lie ahead?

None of the traditional religions provides an adequate basis as we seek answers to these questions. We have outgrown them. Much the same can be said of the approaches of the classical philosophers, whose wisdom, however valid in earlier eras, is of only limited relevance today. And science alone does not provide the kinds of answers we need. It tells us a lot about ourselves and our current condition. But we have to interpret what it tells us when we try to decide what to do with that information. When we start interpreting, we have to rely on value judgments that we know are time and culture-bound. If the old values aren't adequate, what standards *do* we employ?

At least, we start with a fairly clean slate. The more progressive and creative thinkers among us don't have to start by explaining why the systems we inherited don't work. That has already been done by the rebellious philosophers and artists of the early and mid-twentieth century, as I described in chapter 20.

Progressive Humanism is a modest attempt at creating a new framework for the future. None of its constituent parts is original. The same can be said for many of its more complex components. It is the overall design that I hope will strike the reader as having something to offer.

The Progressive Humanist defines progress as any change that a specific social group in a specific time and location considers desirable and causes to happen. It does not involve any absolute sense of direction or purpose, any more than biological evolution does. It involves no absolute values, only those of the group concerned. It is, for human societies, what evolution is for biological life. It is the process that is responsible for the gradual increase in complexity and functionality of human social groups from the dawn of the Paleolithic era up to the present.

The believer in Progressive Humanism believes that progress is not only possible but even, in the long run, inevitable. It is what confers purpose on our existence. An equally important article of faith is that humanity, all humanity, is what it is all about. We are a team in which every individual human being is important.

These, then, are the two bedrock assumptions of the Progressive Humanist: the inevitability of progress, and the prime importance of humanity. Life can be seen as a continuing effort to balance them and to steer a course that violates neither. Together they will, I submit, serve humanity well in the decades to come. Certainly they will serve us better than most of the outdated or superseded assumptions that guide us now. We are confused and irresolute because the answers traditional guidance is giving us are conflicting and largely dysfunctional. We need a new and clearer sense of who we are and where we are going. We need a new framework.

Epilogue

THE MILLENNIAL VIEW

It's a hard pull climbing Shivpuri, the mountain that forms the northern rim of Kathmandu Valley. The locals don't call it a mountain; for them, it is just a hill, since it is merely the closest of a series of increasingly high ridges leading north to the "real" mountains, the Himals or snow peaks. And it is true that from other parts of the valley, on a clear day, you can see the Himals on the northern horizon. But we who lived in Kathmandu lived in the shadow of Shivpuri, and it seemed, at 9,000 feet, pretty forbidding in its own right.

I tried to climb Shivpuri several times during my first year or two in Kathmandu, but always tired and quit before I reached the top. Finally, one crisp autumn day, I determined to succeed—and did.

Almost from the beginning, where the path leaves the valley, the trail up Shivpuri corkscrews its way straight up; it curves and twists but seldom levels off to a grade much less than twenty degrees. Hill people on their way to the next valley lope past me, chattering away. From time to time, I catch glimpses of parts of the valley I have been struggling so hard to leave. The higher I ascend, the better the views to the rear. And finally, the trail enters a pine forest and forks. The villagers take the right fork, to the next valley, while I plod on up the other, toward the summit. The forest ends and I look back: the whole valley spreads out before my eyes in a magnificent panorama, towns and villages and paddy fields and little dirt roads winding like ribbons all through them, brown hills to the south and east and west, and beyond them all a murky haze from the north Indian plains.

And then I turn and climb a short gentle slope and see, to the north, the whole central Himalayan massif, a jagged white sky-line averaging well over 20,000 feet in altitude, the most majestic mountains in the world, looming up behind yet another intervening range of brown hills, yet another series of terraces and villages and mountain trails. Yes, the long climb was worth it, many times over.

This memory serves me well. It provides a striking analogy to what I believe is happening right now to humanity as a whole as we enter a new millennium. We've done a lot of tough climbing; for the last couple of thousand generations or more we've been slogging away, rewarded only intermittently by the occasional backward look at patches of the scenery we've already traversed, enough to give us a sense that we've come a long way, but not much more. Now, suddenly, it's all coming together, we've reached a point where we can look back and see the whole panorama, bits and pieces missing to be sure, but enough to take in the entire noble sweep of the history and prehistory of our species.

We now, for the first time, have a reasonably complete and

accurate understanding of who we are, and how we came to be that way. It's a marvelous view, a revelation. It's like a child experiencing snow for the first time—except that the sense of wonder is even greater.

We know that we have overcome formidable natural threats to our species, so much so that we now control the planet to a large extent, and continued expansion of our numbers, not survival, has become our number-one problem.

We observe, as we examine the evidence, how human culture has evolved in many different ways in different places and different times. We see how each culture invented its own gods to reinforce its own ethics, morality, and indeed basic identity, and how this enhanced its group's strength and solidarity. Differentiation based on physical appearance, language, and material culture also reinforced tribal particularity. We observe how this differentiation of cultures has led to intergroup warfare and other forms of competition that in turn resulted in our incredibly speedy conquest of our planet.

But we have arrived at a position where it isn't enough just to look back and marvel at how far we have come. Let's turn around, climb that last short slope, and look ahead.

We see one world, one all-embracing humanity, where tribal variations haven't necessarily been abolished but where tribal instincts have been turned around so that they work for the species as a whole, not just a particular group, and a panhuman Golden Rule prevails.

We see a world where we have learned to manage planet Earth, not just overcome it, where our numbers are in balance with Earth's carrying capacity, allowing us the privacy and freedom we need, and allowing us to share Earth's bounty with the other animals and plants that have been here during our formative years.

We see a world where we have achieved the goal of equal opportunity for every human being, where no child's talents, whatever they may be, shall be wasted.

We see a world where we acknowledge that the future of humanity is a human responsibility, not that of some deity worshiped by past generations before we came this far up the slope. We have faith not in any deity but in the future of humankind, and in our ability to create that future.

And that is the view of the next series of foothills, the view we see unfolding before us in the middle distance. No, we have not yet raised our eyes to the snowpeaks that lie beyond. But we can see them, shimmering on the skyline, beckoning us with still unimaginable glories. They tell us that the long saga of our species will not end when we have achieved the millennial goal of a unified and purposeful species; even then, the journey will have only begun.

What higher purpose can there be in life, for those who share this millennial view, than to persuade those laggards down below us to pull up their socks, climb the last few feet, and share it with us?

INDEX